Physical Characteristics of the Bernese Mountain Dog

(from the American Kennel Club breed standard)

Topline: Level from the withers to the croup.

Body: The back is broad and firm. The loin is strong. The croup is broad and smoothly rounded to the tail insertion.

Tail: Bushy; carried low when in repose. The bones in the tail should feel straight and should reach to the hock joint or below.

Color and Markings: Tri-colored. The ground color is jet black. The markings are rich rust and clear white. Symmetry of markings is desired.

Coat: Thick, moderately long and slightly wavy or straight. It has a bright natural sheen.

Hindquarters: The thighs are broad, strong and muscular. The stifles are moderately bent and taper smoothly into the hocks. The hocks are well let down and straight as viewed from the rear. Feet are compact and turn neither in nor out.

Size: Measured at the withers, dogs are 25 to 27.5 inches; bitches are 23 to 26 inches.

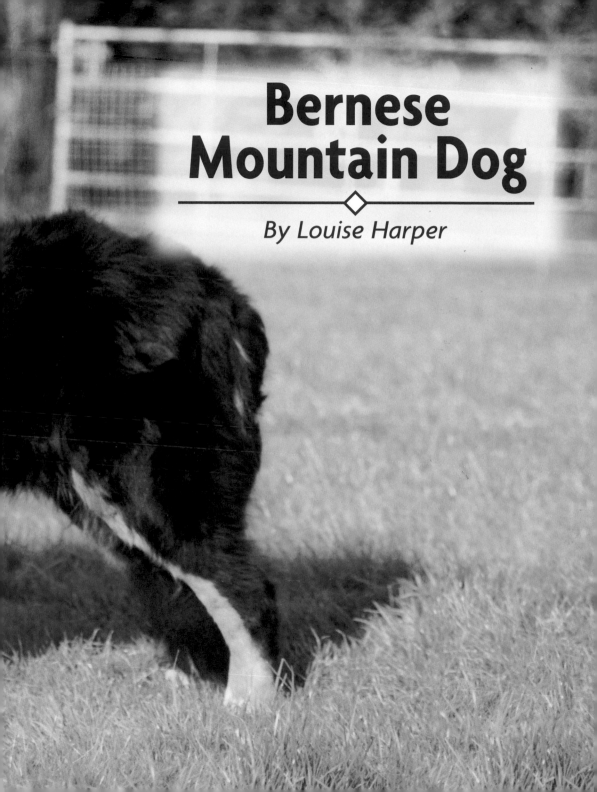

Bernese
Mountain Dog

◇

By Louise Harper

Contents

KENNEL CLUB BOOKS: BERNESE MOUNTAIN DOG
ISBN: 1-59378-289-6

Copyright © 2000 • **Revised American Edition: Copyright © 2004**
Kennel Club Books, Inc., 308 Main Street, Allenhurst, NJ 07711 USA
Cover Design Patented: US 6,435,559 B2 • Printed in South Korea

Photographs by:
Carol Ann Johnson and Michael Trafford
with additional photos by
Norvia Behling, T.J. Calhoun, Carolina Biological Society, Doskocil, Isabelle Français, James Hayden-Yoav, James R. Hayden, RBP, Bill Jonas, Dwight R. Kuhn, Dr. Dennis Kunkel, Mikki Pet Products, Phototake, Jean Claude Revy, Alice Roche, Dr. Andrew Spielman and Karen Taylor.

Illustrations by Patricia Peters.

Bernese Mountain Dogs share their eye-catching Swiss tri-coloration, complemented by wonderful personalities and great physical strength. Although originally bred for working purposes, most Bernese Mountain Dogs today serve as pets to adoring owners.

BERNESE MOUNTAIN DOG

ORIGIN AND DEVELOPMENT OF THE BREED IN SWITZERLAND

To discover the origin of the Bernese Mountain Dog, we must travel centuries back in time and search the mountains and the remote valleys of the Swiss hinterlands where the breed originated. Forebears of this popular Swiss dog lived and worked among the Celtic farmers of those early times, protecting both humans and livestock from natural predators.

Early history tells us that, around 1000 AD, Swiss settlers had carved out a peaceful existence on the mountainsides, co-existing harmoniously with nature and her beasts. History also reveals that the more prosperous families kept large Swiss working dogs as protectors of the field and home. The poorer farmers, unable to feed large animals with prodigious appetites, kept smaller dogs in keeping with their meager budgets.

Supporting that theory, writer Conrad Gessner wrote in 1523: "Some of the big and strong dogs are especially trained to stay around the houses and stables in the fields. They must protect the cattle from danger. Some guard the cattle, some the fields and some the houses. Other dogs are trained to protect people. They must contend after murderers and other mean people. They must be fierce and big and strong, as they must fight against warriors in their armour."

It is apparent that their dogs were bred to perform specific tasks, although selective breeding was not yet common among the people of that time. For many generations, herding cattle was the most important duty of every mountain dog. Additionally, the dogs were used as guard dogs to give warning at the approach of wild animals, such as bears and wolves, as well as predatory humans who came to steal at any price. Although few modern dogs show evidence of these ancient instincts, many specimens of mountain dog still retain those herding and guarding instincts in their blood.

In those days, the measure of any dog that was kept purely as

Views of Berne, Switzerland, for which the Bernese Mountain Dog is named. Berne is the capital city of Switzerland. It was named after the wild bears that lived in the area. Berne was founded in 1191 and is considered to be one of the landmark cities of the world.

working household inventory was in its ability and usefulness as a herder and as a protector of people and property. Conventional companion dogs were considered a useless luxury, as they were merely extra mouths to feed.

In about 1850, the mountain dogs took on another task as a working group. Local Swiss farmers, long known for making superior cheeses, built cheese plants, called cheeseries, and many used their dogs to pull carts loaded with milk cans to supply their businesses.

Prior to that time, the breed had no formal name. They were simply known as farm dogs, butchers' dogs or cheesery dogs. Understandably, they became known by their specific markings—those with white rings around their necks were not surprisingly called "Ringgi," dogs with distinct blazes down their face were known as "Blassi" and those with little white markings on their faces were known as "Bari," which means "little bear." The Bari were also known as the "Gelbackler," a name denoting "yellow cheeks"; and those dogs with tan markings over their eyes were called "Vieraugli," a name which means "four eyes."

Given the expedient nature of the mountain dogs, the demand for them was great. They were widely bought and sold, and, in

GENUS *CANIS*

Dogs and wolves are members of the genus *Canis*. Wolves are known scientifically as *Canis lupus* while dogs are known as *Canis domesticus*. Dogs and wolves are known to interbreed. The term "canine" derives from the Latin word *Canis*. The term "dog" has no scientific basis but has been used for thousands of years. The origin of the word "dog" has never been authoritatively ascertained.

the mid-1800s, the center of such trade found itself at the Durrbachler Gasthaus. Not coincidentally, the breed soon became known as the Durrbachler, so named after that central trading post.

Around the same time, the St. Bernard's popularity was rising, thus diminishing interest in the mountain breeds. The massive St. Bernard, also Swiss in origin, with his uniform coloration, captivated the dog fancy, and the tri-colored Swiss mountain dog remained steadfast only in those remote areas where farmers and craftsmen required the use of the dogs to obtain sustenance.

In 1883 the Swiss Kennel Club was formed. Their first dog show offered a class for the St.

Bernard as well as other Swiss hounds, but did not recognize the mountain dogs. Interest in the St. Bernard continued to grow, with correspondingly less attention paid to the lowly mountain dogs.

A major change in attitude occurred in 1892, when Franz Schertenleib, an innkeeper from Burgdorf, regenerated interest in the old-fashioned type of farmer's dog. Inspired by his father's tales of the breed, he embarked on a mission to preserve the dogs for future generations. Schertenleib scoured Berne for suitable breed candidates, and his quest soon sparked greater interest among proponents of other similar breeds of dog.

Most certainly the greatest impact on the evolution of the breed came in the early 1900s through the efforts of Albert Heim, a professor of geology, who

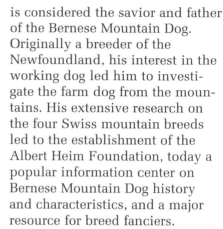

is considered the savior and father of the Bernese Mountain Dog. Originally a breeder of the Newfoundland, his interest in the working dog led him to investigate the farm dog from the mountains. His extensive research on the four Swiss mountain breeds led to the establishment of the Albert Heim Foundation, today a popular information center on Bernese Mountain Dog history and characteristics, and a major resource for breed fanciers.

In 1904 several breed fanciers convinced the Swiss Kennel Club (SKC) to open a class for the Durrbachler at a show to be held in Berne. Six dogs and one bitch were shown, and the course of the breed was set when four of those dogs were registered with the SKC the following year. During the next ten years, Durrbachlers of unknown parentage were granted entry in the Swiss Stud Book, with each entry requiring the approval of one of three recognized experts on the breed: the mountain-dog enthusiast Franz Schertenleib; another experienced breeder, Gottlfried Mumenthaler; and a veterinarian from Langnethal, Dr. Scheidegger.

These three fanciers, joined by the illustrious Albert Heim, formed the first breed organization, calling it the Schweizerischer Durrbach Klub. As a founding member, Heim suggested that all of the tri-color

ANCIENT ANCESTORS

Twentieth-century excavations in the Swiss mountain area have uncovered the skeletal remains of large dogs dating from the Bronze and Iron Ages. These dogs are assumed to be direct ancestors of today's Swiss mountain dogs. Those discoveries also bring into question another older theory that suggests that, many generations earlier, these same dogs may have been bred to the ancient Mollossus dogs of Roman times.

SWISS COUSINS

According to the FCI, there are four recognized breeds of Swiss mountain dogs: the Bernese Mountain Dog, the Greater Swiss Mountain Dog, the Appenzeller and the Entlebucher. The American Kennel Club, only recognizes the Berner and the Greater Swiss. The breeds differ in size, coat length and type, all sharing the renowned Swiss tri-color pattern.

The smallest of the quartet is the Entlebucher, who stands under 20 inches and weighs between 55 and 66 pounds. The Entlebucher is the only bobtail member of the family. The Appenzeller stands 19 to 23 inches high and weighs between 49 and 55 pounds. The giant of the quartet is the Greater Swiss or "Swissy," whose ancestry is likely the most ancient and is linked to the St. Bernard. The Swissy is called the Grosser Schweizer Sennenhund at home. The Swissy stands as tall as 23.5 to 28.5 inches and weighs around 130 pounds. All three breeds are smooth coated, unlike the Bernese.

The Entlebucher.

The Appenzeller.

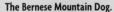
The Bernese Mountain Dog.

The Greater Swiss Mountain Dog.

Durrbach dogs fall under the same designation and he persuaded the club members to name the breed the Berner Sennenhund, honoring the town in which the breed had proliferated. The name was actually inappropriate to the origin and duty of the dog, as the literal translation means "Bernese alpine (mountain) herdsman's dog," and the Durrbach dogs came from the lowlands. However, the club, after some disagreement, approved the name change. Pursuant to that, the club also became known as the Berner Sennenhund Klub.

By the year 1908, interest in the Bernese had increased significantly, and that year the show at Langenthal sported a total of 21 entries. Two years later, in 1910, there were 42 dogs at a show in Berne. Entries continued to climb, and on April 24, 1910, the club show in Burgdorf made breed history with a record-setting entry of 107 Berners.

Professor Heim was the esteemed judge at that Burgdorf show. Many of the entries he inspected had color variations that were no longer desirable in the breed, as well as coats that were untypical of a true breed representative. Heim was kind but honest in his criticism and disqualified several dogs on the basis of their coats and markings. He also counseled the exhibitors

> **VOO-DEW!**
> In the remote farming areas of Switzerland, the natives believed that Bernese with black feet and double dewclaws had supernatural powers to ward off evil spirits.

about producing higher quality animals that would contribute to the betterment of the breed.

Because Heim was held in such high regard within the breeding community, his words and the standards he set had great impact on the breeders, convincing them to improve on appearance and temperament and to eliminate poor specimens from their breeding programs. Although some differences in color and markings still continued, the show produced many good specimens who were ultimately admitted to the Stud Book. Breeders took note, which ultimately enhanced their breeding programs in their quest for a more uniform-type dog.

Those efforts also served to define the Berner's characteristics as distinct from the three other Alpine mountain breeds: the Greater Swiss Mountain Dog, the Appenzeller and the Entlebucher, with the Greater Swiss (or "Swissy") sharing a common past with the St. Bernard. While all four breeds are "workaholic" dogs with native herding instincts,

Berners have been employed as draft dogs and cart pullers for generations. In an exhibition, this Berner is celebrating his heritage by pulling a ceremonial cart.

there are major differences in type, size and coat. And while all four share the same placid, friendly disposition, there are still subtle differences in temperament. The Bernese and the Swissy, the larger of the four breeds, are today by far the better known of the Alpine breeds, and they remain more popular than the smaller Appenzeller and the Entlebucher.

Throughout the first decade of the 20th century, the Bernese trailed the Appenzeller and the St. Bernard in popularity. Gradually, however, the breed became more uniform as more farmers and breeders continued to show their dogs. Breed club membership climbed to 40 members, with greater numbers of good dogs being shown on the bench. By 1917 the Berner had gained considerable ground and finally surpassed the Appenzeller in registrations; 20 years later, breed registrations also exceeded those of the St. Bernard.

Breeding practice throughout the early 1900s was sketchy at best, with many dogs of unknown ancestry used for breeding. However, by 1940 one could find pedigrees with five generations recorded, with little inbreeding in the background. But despite efforts to retain only the best qualities of the breed, correct temperament was still a problem. Thus, club members agreed it might be necessary to introduce another breed into the gene pool.

About that time, nature intervened and provided a solution. A Bernese bitch named Christine v. Lux became pregnant when a Newfoundland dog named Pluto v. Erlengut jumped the fence and accidentally mated with her. She whelped seven pups—three bitches and four dogs—on December 21, 1948, and it was no small surprise that all the puppies looked like Newfoundlands. Speculation was rampant about whether this breeding was truly accidental or was in fact a deliberate experiment to inject new blood into the Bernese breed.

Of the seven pups, one pup was retained for breeding. This was a bitch named Babette, who was given to club member Dr. Hauser for future use. Babette matured with the typical temperament and conformation of a Newfoundland. When she turned three years of age, she was bred with a Berner named Aldo v. Tieffurt, a breeding that produced six live and two stillborn pups. Four of the pups were incorrectly marked, with only one male and one female carrying Bernese markings. The bitch was named Christine v. Schwarzwassserbachli and was given to Herr Mischler, the president of the breed club at the time.

Mischler bred Christine at nine months of age to a Bernese named Osi v. Allenluften, who was a proven producer. The pairing produced five pups, with only one male and one female surviving. The male, Alex, grew into a superb representative of the breed and won numerous awards on the bench, becoming an International Champion as well as the World Champion in 1956.

It was no surprise, then, that many Bernese breeders came to Alex for stud service. Throughout

BRAIN AND BRAWN

Since dogs have been inbred for centuries, their physical and mental characteristics are constantly being changed to suit man's desires for drafting, retrieving, scenting, guarding and warming their masters' laps. During the past 150 years, dogs have been judged according to physical characteristics as well as functional abilities. Few breeds can boast a genuine balance between physique, working ability and temperament.

his lifetime, he was bred to a wide variety of bitches, producing 51 litters and imprinting his offspring with many desirable Bernese characteristics. Over time, many breeders developed line-breeding programs to capitalize on the fine qualities that were produced in the Alex matings.

THE BERNER IN ITS HOMELAND

Entering the 21st century, the Bernese Mountain Dog remains one of the most popular breeds in Switzerland, and the Schweiz-erischer Klub is one of the largest breed clubs in the country. The club maintains strict control over breeding practices through a series of assessments called "Ankrung," which are held several times a year throughout the country. Officials of the breed club act as assessors to judge breeding candidates for tempera-ment and conformity to the breed standard, and only those dogs who are considered worthy speci-mens of the breed are passed as fit for breeding.

Hip status is also an important criterion for breeding. Because hip dysplasia is a serious genetic problem in the breed, only dogs with grades of 0 or 1 are passed as suitable for breeding. The Swiss Kennel Club also will not issue a pedigree to the offspring of any dog who is considered a poor specimen of the breed.

"AS THE FRENCH SAY..."
In France and in the French part of Switzerland, the Bernese Mountain Dog is called the *Bouvier Bernois*.

The Swiss Kennel Club main-tains rigid control over the breed-ing community and permits breeders to produce only one litter from any bitch in any single year, with only six puppies allowed to survive from each litter. Throughout all of Switzer-land, whenever a litter is born, the breeder must inform the area puppy controller, called a "Wurfkontrolle." An experienced breeder who is also a member of the breed club is assigned to oversee each area's breeding programs. If more than six pups are born, the litter must be culled.

The reasons for culling are in the best interest of the breed. The Swiss feel strongly that only the very best specimens of any breed should be kept and bred, which charges the breeder with carefully selecting which puppies should be culled. There is also natural concern for the health of the dam and general agreement that rearing six pups places minimal stress on a nursing mother. Commendably, the breed club also worries about overpopulation and the risks of puppy mills and other irresponsi-ble breeders that are an unfortunate by-product of popularity. Few breeders in Switzerland oppose these sentiments; most willingly subscribe to these breeding limitations.

The Wurfkontrolle also assist novice breeders in culling their pups as well as in other breeding issues. The culling process results in selection for correct size and markings, and the Swiss believe that will help to ensure the future quality of the breed. Pups cannot be sold until they are least eight weeks old.

The Bernese Mountain Dog is greatly revered and protected in its native Switzerland. The breed club is intensely committed to preserving the working ability of the Bernese. In fact, the entire dog community is committed to ensuring the future of the breed. Training clubs abound and many of these regularly conduct working tests. Swiss veterinarians go to great lengths to educate breeders and owners about health issues. The breed clubs publish bulletins to keep the Bernese Mountain Dog

The Berner is still extremely popular in its native Switzerland, where breeders work diligently to produce outstanding bitches and dogs for their breeding programs.

community informed on breed issues and activities. Breed popularity elsewhere in the world has only intensified the Swiss determination to breed the best Berners possible.

Swiss breeders have worked consistently to produce outstanding dogs and bitches in their breeding programs. The use of Alex v. Angstorf had a profound effect on the success enjoyed by many kennels. Frau Tschanz is a sterling example of Alex's influence. Under her Dursrutti prefix, she has produced many generations of champions through a carefully constructed long-range breeding program that incorporated Alex's bloodlines.

Amadeus Krauchi is another successful Swiss breeder who is famous throughout the US and Great Britain for his von Nesselacker Bernese. Superior specimens of the breed, they won at many shows and produced equally well through the late 20th century.

We saw another world-class winner in the famous Asso v. Hogerbuur, who for many years was housed at the von Grunenmatt kennels, founded by Ernst Schlucter. Asso's show-ring charisma was legendary—he always thrilled both judges and spectators. He continued his legacy of excellence as a working dog in the field. Another Grunenmatt Berner, named Xodi, went to

Canada to become one of the foundation Bernese in that country. Schlucter also sent Fox v. Grunenmatt to Great Britain to improve and sustain their breeding stock.

Another Bernese legend, Herr Iseli, who was a well-known breed authority and judge held in high regard, founded his von Sumiswald kennel in 1923. That kennel continued through Iseli's son, who presided as President of the Swiss breed club from 1971 to 1980. Iseli also exported his three-year-old Senta v. Sumiswald to England in 1936. Co-owned by Mrs. Perry and Mrs. Patterson, Senta was the first Bernese to be imported to Great Britain.

THE BERNESE MOUNTAIN DOG IN THE UNITED STATES

Although there is documentation of two Bernese having been imported to America in 1926, it would be another ten years before the breed was accepted and recognized in the US. In 1935 Mr. Shadow of Louisiana read an article on the Bernese written by Swiss breeder Mrs. Egg Leach for the *American Kennel Gazette*. Mr. Shadow had become enchanted with the breed during his youth, and he contacted Mrs. Leach, subsequently arranging the importation of a male, Quell v. Tiergarten, and a female, Friday v. Haslenbach, the following year. These two dogs became the first imports of the breed to be recognized by the American Kennel Club (AKC) when the registry accepted the breed in 1937. The Bernese Mountain Dog and the Greater Swiss Mountain Dog are the only two Swiss mountain breeds that are recognized by the American Kennel Club.

Mr. Shadow was steadfast in his commitment to his Bernese and unswerving in his efforts to promote the breed in the United States. Those efforts were thwarted by the Second World War, however, and for the next ten years Mr. Shadow's dogs were the only Bernese to be registered with the AKC.

During the next two decades, breed growth was slow. The vast geography of breed enthusiasts interfered with propagating the Bernese in many parts of the country. But, by the late 1960s, there was enough interest to warrant the formation of a breed club. The Bernese Mountain Dog Club of America was launched in 1968 with just eight members. Within that first year, membership grew to 33, a newsletter was published and the club held its first "fun" match. To their credit, the club has established a Working Dog Award and a Working Dog Excellent Award to honor those dogs who prove to possess the desired working ability of the breed. The breed has enjoyed a modest but steady rise in popularity, and breed registration with the AKC has grown to over 2,000 annually.

THE BERNESE MOUNTAIN DOG IN GREAT BRITAIN

Mrs. Perry of the Kobe kennels and Mrs. Patterson of the Fontana kennels were Samoyed breeders who decided to establish the Bernese in their native England. After acquiring Senta v. Sumiswald in 1936, the first Bernese to be imported into England, their next breed acquisitions arrived the following year, all under two years of age. These were a male named Quell, a bitch named Nelly and an in-whelp bitch named Laura, all bred by Fritz Stalder of the Haslebacher kennel; another male, Dani, bred by Herr Haslebacher; and a third bitch, Cacilie, who was bred by Herr Schmid. Laura whelped four pups while still in quarantine in 1937; the pups were named Alex, Bruno, Nero and Berna. These pups were the first Bernese to be born in Great Britain, and they went on to establish more of the foundation of the breed in that country. Mrs. Perry bred Dani and Nelly the following year, thus helping to establish other Bernese breeding kennels.

The Second World War interrupted Bernese breeding programs. Just as with many other breeds of dog, the few Bernese pups and adults then on

The Berner is agile and fast. It is still used for herding in Switzerland and exhibits fair endurance for its large size.

the island were given away to homes who could afford to feed and care for them, and the breed literally disappeared during that time.

The Bernese remained virtually nonexistent until about two decades later, when Mrs. Irene Creigh, a breeder of Mastiffs, discovered a charming-looking dog called the Bernese Mountain Dog in a photograph sent to her by a Mastiff client in Switzerland. Mrs. Creigh collaborated with her friend, Mrs. Mabel Coates, and the two women imported two Bernese: a male pup from Herr Mathez and a young bitch from Herr Kobel.

While these two imports were still in quarantine, a rabies alert created a freeze on quarantined

dogs and none was permitted to leave after the normal quarantine period had expired. Mrs. Coates arranged for the two dogs to be mated during their prolonged confinement. They were born under Mrs. Coates's Nappa kennel affix. Three of the pups went to serious breeders and went on to become foundation dogs for three successful Bernese kennels.

One of the three, Black Magic of Nappa, was purchased and

GROUP WINNER

In 1980, a Bernese Mountain Dog named Eng. Ch. Folkdance at Forgeman was the first of his breed to ever win the Working Dog Group at the famous Crufts Dog Show in England.

campaigned by Joyce Collis. Although never widely used at stud, "Berni" became a high-profile representative for the Bernese when he appeared on the popular children's television program *Magpie*. Berni was later shipped to Mr. Dick Schneider in the United States, where he won Best of Breed at his first show in that country. His career was unfortunately short-lived, however, when he died of heat stroke the following year.

Meanwhile, it was Mrs. Creigh who had the greater impact on the Berner's proliferation in Great Britain. She continued to expand her breeding program, using the two original imports, Dora and Oro, as the foundation for her stock. Her dedication was responsible for the founding of the Bernese Mountain Dog Club of England, which was later renamed the Bernese Mountain Dog Club of Great Britain. She served as secretary to the club and also started a breed newsletter while in that office.

The Bernese breed club was launched in 1971 with 25 members. They held their first Open Show eight years later in 1979, to which they invited Herr Krauchi and Herr Iseli from Switzerland to assess the dogs that were being shown. Again Mrs. Creigh's contribution to the breed was evident, when both Best in Show and Best Bitch in Assessment were taken by Ch.

Kisumu Bonne Esperance of Mill-wire, a bitch she had bred and sold to Carol Lilliman. The success of holding an assessment at the show prompted the club to do so every four years, so this event was repeated at shows in 1983 and in 1987. Today the national breed club boasts over 700 members and holds two Open Shows and a Championship Show, supplementing those events with additional assess-ments, working-dog events and educational seminars.

From the 1980s came the Bernese Breeders Association of Great Britain, a group of breeders and fanciers who set about to educate and distribute informa-tion on the breed. The club also sponsors educational seminars throughout the country and publishes a popular club maga-zine called *Oasis*. The club's dedi-cation to the betterment of the breed has made great strides in the continued interest and improvement of the Bernese Mountain Dog in Great Britain.

During the last decade of the 1900s, several Bernese clubs were formed to cater to Berner owners and enthusiasts in specific regions of Great Britain: the Scottish Bernese Mountain Dog Club, the Northern Bernese Mountain Dog Club and the Southern Bernese Mountain Dog Club, which serves fanciers from the midlands to the southern coast.

The Bernese Mountain Dog makes a confident and attractive show dog. More and more Berners are appearing in dog shows, proving that the breed's popularity is ever increasing.

CHARACTERISTICS OF THE
BERNESE MOUNTAIN DOG

IS THE BERNESE FOR YOU?
The Bernese is a striking, tri-colored dog, large in size, with a most amiable disposition. He is intelligent and strong, with the natural agility to perform the draft and droving work for which he was originally bred and used in his native Switzerland. He is a self-confident and good-natured dog, calm and alert, and, while he may appear aloof to strangers, he is steadfast, loyal and affectionate within his family unit. He does best as a house dog, as he is blest with a low activity level when indoors and a strong need to be near his family. He is happiest just being near his loved ones.

Given that propensity, the Bernese makes a poor kennel dog and will not thrive, indeed will be most unhappy, without human companionship. If left untended or unsupervised, he will be bored and become troublesome when not assigned a specific chore. A large yard is not sufficient in and of itself. The adult mountain dog needs long daily walks, at least an hour in length, to keep mentally

Even though the Berner has, historically, been a working dog, he does brilliantly as a house dog. He still requires exercise and mental stimulation to stay in prime condition.

and physically fit, although the Bernese under one year of age should have limited exercise to prevent damage to his immature skeletal structure.

Although the guarding ability is greatly diminished in the modern Bernese, he shows excellent judgment and will make every effort to guard and protect his human family. He also makes a good watchdog and will warn at the approach of a stranger or intruder. The possessive Berner will bark at anyone who invades his territory and hold them at bay, but only extreme action would provoke the dog into real aggression. He is considered totally reliable as a house pet and family companion.

The Bernese's herding instincts color everything he does. A mountain dog will herd everyone and guard anything. Although he adores children, his size and playful exuberance could easily overwhelm a small child. And despite his gentle nature, he can become unruly without proper training.

The Bernese has a strong desire, indeed an indefatigable need, to work, and thus is constantly looking for a challenge or a job to do. Adaptable to many tasks, they are biddable, willing and eager to please. They will never challenge an owner's authority if they are properly schooled at an early age.

KEEPING YOUR BERNER BURNING
Owners need to keep this active pure-bred busy and feeling productive. Here's a list of some possibilities for dog and owner:

- backpacking and hiking
- carting and weight pulling events
- obedience competition
- agility trials or obedience trials
- Versatility and Working tests
- dog shows
- camping
- search and rescue
- therapy dog, visiting hospitals and homes

Berners also possess a great sense of humor and often display clownish behavior in order to be the center of attention. They can, however, sometimes have a stubborn streak, which may lead them to be somewhat manipulative.

Surely the greatest disadvantage to owning a Bernese Mountain Dog is his brief life expectancy. Most live only seven to eight years, with a fortunate few surviving up to ten years of age.

ACTIVITIES FOR THE BERNESE MOUNTAIN DOG

There is no doubt that a Bernese is happiest when he has a job or when he is performing a task with or for his master. In their native Switzerland, as well as other countries throughout the world, many Bernese still thrive as working farm dogs—pulling carts, tending livestock and guarding their property and human families.

Berners in Switzerland also serve as rescue dogs, especially in the mountainous areas of the country, where they are specially trained for disaster work in avalanche and earthquake emergencies. Some also work as ambulance dogs, locating injured people in crowds or wooded areas. The Bernese loves to follow scents, and so he is particularly well suited for tracking lost people. In addition to the public-service element of rescue work, Bernese now participate in rescue trials, where they can display their talents as proficient search and rescue teams.

In most countries, however, working tests offer the best opportunity for the Bernese to enjoy his heritage. Kennel clubs and breed clubs host a variety of enjoyable events to test and challenge the skills of many breeds of working dog.

Carting is the special passion of the Bernese, so it is no surprise that this activity is extremely popular with the dog as well as his like-minded owner. Both Switzerland and Sweden conduct draft-dog trials, with special

> **DO YOU WANT TO LIVE LONGER?**
> If you like to volunteer, it is wonderful if you can take your dog to a nursing home once a week for several hours. The elder community loves to have a dog with which to visit, and often your dog will bring a bit of companionship to someone who is lonely or somewhat detached from the world. You will be not only bringing happiness to someone else but also keeping your dog busy—and we haven't even mentioned the fact that it has been discovered that volunteering helps to increase your own longevity!

courses designed specifically for them. The dogs' appetite for draft work is so strong that owners have difficulty controlling their dogs' impatience and enthusiasm during the harnessing and at the starting line. The harnesses and carts are a major part of the carting spectacle, with beautiful handwork on the harnesses and elaborate decorations on the carts.

The Bernese Mountain Dog Club of America sponsors draft tests, including a series of exercises designed to challenge and develop the breed's natural hauling ability. As a leisure activity just for fun, most Berners in Switzerland and Germany have been shown in working harness at parades, club events and other public outings.

Showing your Bernese Mountain Dog in conformation can be an enjoyable and fulfilling activity for both dog and owner. However, there is more to this sport than merely trotting about the show ring with your dog. Whether you are a hobbyist or fierce competitor, your dog's physical attributes and breed-specific qualities, temperament and attitude, coat condition and grooming techniques, gait and movement, as well as handler expertise, all contribute to your success in the dog-show game. If you are serious about competing in the show ring, you should first consult with your breeder or another experienced Bernese owner. It is also wise to acquaint yourself with other show fanciers to learn and understand the rules and finer points of this highly competitive canine activity.

Currently the sport of agility has become a top interest of the dog fancy; it is especially popular with owners of working and/or athletic dogs. Agility trials set up timed obstacle courses, each one designed for different-sized dogs. Contestants must navigate over, under, through and around tunnels, jumps, bridges and other obstacles. All breeds of dog are eligible to participate, although larger breeds such as the Bernese should not attempt jumping during their first year or two of growth, when their bone structure is still forming and quite vulnera-

ble. The AKC forbids training any dog for agility trials before the age of one year.

Weight pulling is a sport that comes natural to draft dogs like the Berner, Swissy, Rottweiler and other muscular dogs, though any dog can participate in these trials. Weight pulls are sponsored by three organizations in the US, the International Weight Pull Association (IWPA), the United Kennel Club (UKC) and the National Kennel Club (NKC). Formed in 1984, the IWPA is the only organization specifically formed to promote the sport of weight

Bernese Mountain Dog puppies are receptive to children and welcome their attention. This pup is enjoying a rest on a cart with his young friend.

Pulling a cart is a natural task for the Berner. For owners interested in training their Berners for draft work, there are clubs that promote trials and special meets for owners and their dogs.

pulling in the spirit of the working heritage of individual breeds. Weight pulls are good exercise for dogs and lots of safe fun for both dogs and spectators. Safety is always the main emphasis at a weight pull.

At these events, the dog who can pull the most weight over a 16-foot course is the winner. The dog must show his own willingness to pull, something at which the Berner naturally excels. The dogs compete by pulling wheeled carts or on a rail, and sled dogs compete

on snow with sleds. Hundreds of dogs compete in these events, and there over 100 pulls held each year. Information on events near your home can be found on the Internet at www.iwsp.net.

Dogs are divided by weight, which is divided into six classes: up to 35 pounds; 36-60 pounds; 61 to 80 pounds; 81 to 100 pounds; 101-120 pounds, and over 121 pounds. The Berner can weigh anywhere from 75 to 100 pounds. The IWPA offers three different Working Dog certificates to dogs who can pull certain amounts based on their body weights, usually six or seven times their weight. For example, the NKC indicates that starting weights may not exceed 400 pounds for a 60-pound dog and 500 pounds for an 80-pound dog. The NKC offers three titles to winners: WPT1 (12 times body weight), WPT2 (18 times) and WPT3 (23 times). Getting involved with weight pulls can be a real joy for dog and owner alike.

OWNING A BERNESE MOUNTAIN DOG

Despite his lovable appearance and disposition, the Bernese is not the ideal dog for everyone. Potential owners would be wise to ask themselves these important questions before adding a Bernese to their family.

1. Consider your lifestyle: would a Bernese enjoy or thrive if included in your daily schedule? Do you have time to raise a puppy properly?

2. Does every family member agree that this dog should be a member of the family?

3. How will you care for the puppy and, later, the adult dog, and what arrangements do you plan to make? Who will care for this dog if you become ill or are on vacation?

4. Can one member of the family be with your Bernese for the most part of every day?

5. Will you object to the dust, dirt and hair that a normal Bernese will drag through your home?

6. Do you have enough indoor and outdoor space suitable for this large breed of dog?

7. Does your landlord or homeowner association allow the keeping of large dogs as pets?

8. Can you afford the food, health care, supplies and other costs that come with the dog?

9. Do any family members suffer from allergies to dog hair?

10. Are you committed to all of the above for the next eight to ten years?

Consider the needs of the dog before acquiring a Bernese Mountain Dog. This dog will depend on you for everything from food and water to exercise, entertainment and affection.

BERNESE MOUNTAIN DOG

Every breed that is recognized by a national or international breed registry is judged against what is called a breed standard; that is, a detailed description of the dog's physical characteristics, natural ability and temperament. Most standards were written and approved by the original breed fanciers who initiated the dog's acceptance into the American Kennel Club or other registry. Their goal was to describe the ideal specimen of their breed, and the standard is intended to be a guideline for judging in the show ring. This is equally important as a blueprint for the breeding of future generations of each breed. Without such guidelines, specific inherent breed qualities could be changed, lost or completely eliminated. While it is not possible to produce a perfect specimen of any breed, breeders who respect and understand their standard will continue to select and breed only the best representatives of their particular breed.

THE AMERICAN KENNEL CLUB STANDARD FOR THE BERNESE MOUNTAIN DOG

General Appearance: The Bernese Mountain Dog is a striking, tri-colored, large dog. He is sturdy and balanced. He is intelligent, strong and agile enough to do the draft and droving work for which he was used in the mountainous regions of his origin. Dogs appear masculine, while bitches are distinctly feminine.

Size, Proportion, Substance: Measured at the withers, dogs are 25 to 27.5 inches; bitches are 23 to 26 inches. Though appearing square, Bernese Mountain Dogs are slightly longer in body than they are tall. Sturdy bone is of great importance. The body is full.

BREEDER'S BLUEPRINT

If you are considering breeding your bitch, it is very important that you are familiar with the breed standard. Reputable breeders breed with the intention of producing dogs that are as close as possible to the standard and that contribute to the advancement of the breed. Study the standard for both physical appearance and temperament, and make certain your bitch and your chosen stud dog measure up.

Head: *Expression* is intelligent, animated and gentle. The *eyes* are dark brown and slightly oval in shape with close-fitting eyelids. Inverted or everted eyelids are serious faults. Blue eye color is a disqualification. The *ears* are medium sized, set high, triangular in shape, gently rounded at the tip, and hang close to the head when in repose. When the Bernese Mountain Dog is alert, the ears are brought forward and raised at the base; the top of the ear is level with the top of the skull. The *skull* is flat on top and broad, with a slight furrow and a well-defined, but not exaggerated stop. The *muzzle* is strong and straight. The *nose* is always black. The *lips* are clean and, as the Bernese Mountain Dog is a dry-mouthed breed, the flews are only slightly developed. The *teeth* meet in a scissors bite. An overshot or undershot bite is a serious fault. Dentition is complete.

Neck, Topline, Body: The *neck* is strong, muscular and of medium length. The *topline* is level from the withers to the croup. The *chest* is deep and capacious with well-sprung, but not barrel-shaped, ribs and brisket reaching at least to the elbows. The back is broad and firm. The *loin* is strong. The *croup* is broad and smoothly rounded to the tail insertion. The *tail* is bushy. It should be carried low when in repose. An upward swirl is permissible when the dog is alert, but the tail may never curl or be carried over the back. The bones in the tail should feel straight and should reach to the hock joint or below. A kink in the tail is a fault.

Forequarters: The shoulders are moderately laid back, flat-lying, well-muscled and never loose. The *legs* are straight and strong and the

Head study, showing correct type, structure and proportion.

A dog of correct type, balance and structure with correct color markings.

FAULTS IN PROFILE

Left: Weak foreface, generally lacking bone and substance, long back, soft topline, weak pasterns, flat feet, straight in rear. Mismarked (white on back of neck, no white feet in front).
Right: Short neck, loaded upright shoulders, narrow front, toes out in front, falls away behind and lacks angulation, curl at end of tail. Mismarked (white collar).

elbows are well under the shoulder when the dog is standing. The *pasterns* slope very slightly, but are never weak. *Dewclaws* may be removed. The *feet* are round and compact with well-arched toes.

Hindquarters: The *thighs* are broad, strong and muscular. The *stifles* are moderately bent and taper smoothly into the hocks. The *hocks* are well

let down and straight as viewed from the rear. *Dewclaws* should be removed. *Feet* are compact and turn neither in nor out.

Coat: Thick, moderately long and slightly wavy or straight. It has a bright natural sheen. Extremely curly or extremely dull-looking coats are undesirable. The Bernese Mountain Dog is shown in natural

FAULTS IN PROFILE

Left: Low on leg, front toes turning inward, lacking angulation in rear, loaded shoulders.
Right: Ears set too high, upright shoulders, ewe-necked, dip behind shoulders, arch over loin, long back, tail too long and kinked at end, cowhock. Mismarked (white not separated from black and tan markings on forelegs).

coat and undue trimming is to be discouraged.

Color and Markings: The Bernese Mountain Dog is tri-colored. The ground color is jet black. The markings are rich rust and clear white. Symmetry of markings is desired. Rust appears over each eye, on the cheeks reaching to at least the corner of the mouth, on each side of the chest, on all four legs, and under the tail. There is a white blaze and muzzle band. A white marking on the chest typically forms an inverted cross. The tip of the tail is white. White on the feet is desired but must not extend higher than the pasterns. Markings other than described are to be faulted in direct relationship to the extent of the deviation. White legs or a white collar are serious faults. Any ground color other than black is a disqualification.

Gait: The natural working gait of the Bernese Mountain Dog is a slow trot. However, in keeping with his use in draft and droving work, he is capable of speed and agility. There is good reach in front. Powerful drive from the rear is transmitted through a level back. There is no wasted action. Front and rear legs on each side follow through in the same plane. At increased speed, legs tend to converge toward the center line.

MEETING THE IDEAL

The American Kennel Club defines a standard as: "A description of the ideal dog of each recognized breed, to serve as an ideal against which dogs are judged at shows." This "blueprint" is drawn up by the breed's recognized parent club, approved by a majority of its membership, and then submitted to the AKC for approval.

The AKC states that "An understanding of any breed must begin with its standard. This applies to all dogs, not just those intended for showing." The picture that the standard draws of the dog's type, gait, temperament and structure is the guiding image used by breeders as they plan their programs.

Temperament: Self-confident, alert and good-natured, never sharp or shy. The Bernese Mountain Dog should stand steady, though may remain aloof to the attentions of strangers.

Disqualifications: *Blue eye color; any ground color other than black.*

BERNESE MOUNTAIN DOG

TEMPERAMENT COUNTS

Your selection of a good puppy can be determined by your needs. A show potential or a good pet? It is your choice. Every puppy, however, should be of good temperament. Although show-quality puppies are bred and raised with emphasis on physical conformation, responsible breeders strive for equally good temperament. Do not buy from a breeder who concentrates solely on physical beauty at the expense of personality.

SELECTING YOUR BERNESE PUPPY

Unless you plan to show your Bernese, selecting for health and temperament will be more important than the puppy's conformation or markings. A typical Bernese puppy should look square and solid and should carry a thick fuzzy coat. A teddy-bear-shaped head is preferable to a fox-like appearance. Look for balance and angulation if you are seeking a show potential. Also, well-shaped dark eyes, a straight muzzle, noticeable stop and an outgoing temperament will be pluses for the show pup. Healthy pups will have clear eyes, sound structure and correct dentition. The sire and dam should have the necessary clearances for hips, elbows and eyes. It is also wise to visit with and observe at least one of the parents before committing to a pup.

However, the most important consideration in selecting your Bernese is to obtain him as a pup or at least before about one year of age. As a guarding breed with a strong need to be with his people, the Bernese has difficulty coping with a change in owners later in life. Major late-life changes can make him extremely overanxious, disobedient, rebellious and even aggressive. It is best for both dog and human that bonds be established early in the dog's life.

HEREDITARY DISEASES THAT CONCERN PUPPY BUYERS

The Bernese Mountain Dog, unfortunately, does not enjoy the longevity of many other pure-bred dogs, which is all the more reason for potential owners to be concerned about the breed's hereditary diseases. When you meet with your chosen breeder, you should ask him about the diseases discussed herein.

Responsible breeders screen their dogs for hereditary problems before including them in their breeding programs. Since these problems are passed directly from parents to puppies, whether as carriers or as affected animals, breeders must make screening a priority in their programs. If

the breeder you've selected has no interest or concern in these hereditary diseases, find another breeder. Your investment of time in finding a healthy litter of Bernese puppies can pay off in added years with your beloved pet in the future.

HIP DYSPLASIA (HD)

Hip dysplasia is a hereditary disease that involves abnormal or poor formation of the hip joint. Affecting many large-breed dogs, a mild case of HD can cause painful arthritis in the average housedog, and a severe case can render a working dog useless at his designated task. Diagnosis is made only through x-ray examination by a veterinarian, and in Switzerland and the UK, this may be done only after the dog is at least one year of age.

The breeder should afford you the opportunity to meet the sire and dam of the litter. That the breeder knows his line and the health of each Berner in your puppy's pedigree is a good indication of his ethical practices.

BOY OR GIRL?

An important consideration to be discussed is the sex of your puppy. For a family companion, a bitch may be the better choice, considering the female's inbred concern for all young creatures and her accompanying tolerance and patience. It is always advisable to spay a pet bitch or neuter a pet male, which may guarantee her a longer life.

DO YOU KNOW ABOUT HIP DYSPLASIA?

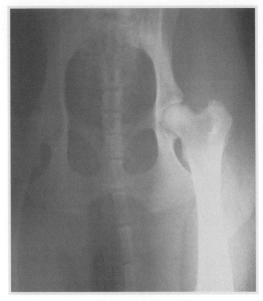

X-ray of a dog with "Good" hips.

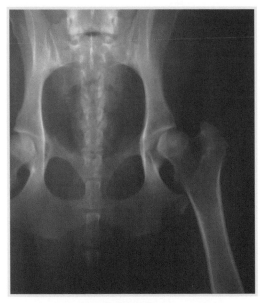

X-ray of a dog with "Moderate" dysplastic hips.

Hip dysplasia is a fairly common condition found in pure-bred dogs. When a dog has hip dysplasia, his hind leg has an incorrectly formed hip joint. By constant use of the hip joint, it becomes more and more loose, wears abnormally and may become arthritic.

Hip dysplasia can only be confirmed with an x-ray, but certain symptoms may indicate a problem. Your dog may have a hip dysplasia problem if he walks in a peculiar manner, hops instead of smoothly runs, uses his hind legs in unison (to keep the pressure off the weak joint), has trouble getting up from a prone position or always sits with both legs together on one side of his body. As the dog matures, he may adapt well to life with a bad hip, but in a few years the arthritis develops and many dogs with hip dysplasia become crippled.

Hip dysplasia is considered an inherited disease and only can be diagnosed definitively by x-ray when the dog is two years old, although symptoms often appear earlier. Some experts claim that a special diet might help your puppy outgrow the bad hip, but the usual treatments are surgical. The removal of the pectineus muscle, the removal of the round part of the femur, reconstructing the pelvis and replacing the hip with an artificial one are all surgical interventions that are expensive, but they are usually very successful. Follow the advice of your veterinarian.

In the US, permanent grades are not assigned until the dog is two years old. Despite the hip guidelines and grading used in breeding programs in the US, 28% of Bernese hip x-rays submitted for evaluation are rated as dysplastic. Berners have the eighth highest incidence of HD in the US, and it is believed that the overall incidence is in reality much higher, since poor hip x-rays are seldom submitted for evaluation.

The Orthopedic Foundation for Animals (OFA) functions as a hip and elbow registry, keeping records on all pure-bred dogs in the country that have been x-rayed for hip dysplasia, elbow dypslasia and many other hereditary diseases. A Bernese Mountain Dog who is 24 months of age or older must be evaluated by three board-certified OFA radiologists, who score the dog's hips as "Excellent," "Good" and "Fair." Any Berner with these passing grades is an eligible candidate for a breeding program. Berners that score "Borderline," "Mild," "Moderate" and "Severe" are not eligible for breeding. The sire and dam of your new puppy should have OFA evaluations, proving that they were eligible for breeding.

Switzerland and Germany have strict rules, allowing only dogs with grades of 0 or 1 to be bred, which has significantly reduced the incidence of HD in those countries. But since the

PUPPY APPEARANCE
Your puppy should have a well-fed appearance but not a distended abdomen, which may indicate worms or incorrect feeding, or both. The body should be firm, with a solid feel. The skin of the abdomen should be pale pink and clean, without signs of scratching or rash. Check the hindlegs to make certain that dewclaws were removed by the breeder.

> ### PEDIGREE VS. REGISTRATION CERTIFICATE
> Too often new owners are confused between these two important documents. Your puppy's pedigree, essentially a family tree, is a written record of a dog's genealogy of three generations or more. The pedigree will show you the names as well as performance titles of all dogs in your pup's background. Your breeder must provide you with a registration application, with his part properly filled out. You must complete the application and send it to the AKC with the proper fee. Every puppy must come from a litter that has been AKC-registered by the breeder, born in the US and from a sire and dam that are also registered with the AKC.
>
> The seller must provide you with complete records to identify the puppy. The AKC requires that the seller provide the buyer with the following: breed; sex, date of birth; litter number (when available); names and registration numbers of the parents; breeder's name; and date sold or delivered.

genetic predisposition is very complex, with many genes involved, there is little likelihood that the disease can be completely eliminated.

OSTEOCHONDRITIS DISSECANS (OCD)

Similar to HD, OCD affects the joints of the shoulder, elbow, hock and stifle, with the shoulder and elbow the most commonly afflicted joints in the Bernese. The disease most commonly affects the growing joints of a puppy under one year of age, and pups will usually exhibit symptoms between five and eight months of age when they come up lame for no apparent reason. The condition is identified through x-ray, and surgery is usually necessary to correct the problem. Males are generally more affected than females, perhaps due to the more rapid growth rate of the male animal. OCD tends to occur in certain families of dogs, with some lines producing higher incidences of the disease. Environmental factors are also thought to contribute to the onset of OCD, with diet and strenuous exercise heavily implicated as offenders. The OFA also keeps a database for OCD records.

HISTIOCYTOSIS

Histiocytosis is the most prevalent cancer in Bernese Mountain Dogs and is a common cause of early death. A histiocyte is a type of white blood cell that comprises part of the dog's immune system. These cells capture bacteria and other foreign material and dispose of them. In histiocytosis, the cells rapidly proliferate and invade major portions of the body tissue. The disease is inherited and there are no known cures or treatments; thus, detection of affected dogs is a priority in Bernese breeding programs. The disease is rare in other breeds but is the most common cancer in the Bernese, comprising 25% of all cancer cases.

Two types of histiocytosis exist, malignant and systemic. Malignant involves the lymph nodes, spleen and liver, and is the more aggressive form of the disease. Onset is sudden and usually leads to death within a few weeks.

Early symptoms include depression, lethargy, loss of appetite and weight loss. Skin abnormalties are not uncommon, especially on the face and limbs. There are no known cures or treatments, so the only recourse is to monitor the dog's quality of life to determine the appropriate time for euthanasia.

HYPOMYELINOGENESIS (TREMBLER)

This inherited disease is a condition caused by a lack of myelin, which is the sheath of insulation material that covers the nerves of the spinal cord. In this disease, the nerve impulses do not travel to the desired destination and instead spread out along the way, causing involuntary trembling.

This condition becomes apparent at 10 to 14 days of age when the pups begin to stand and walk. Affected pups will bobble noticeably and trembling is quite exaggerated, becoming so rapid

ARE YOU PREPARED?
Unfortunately, when a puppy is bought by someone who does not take into consideration the time and attention that dog ownership requires, it is the puppy who suffers when he is either abandoned or placed in a shelter by a frustrated owner. So all of the "home-work" you do in preparation for your pup's arrival will benefit you both. The more informed you are, the more you will know what to expect and the better equipped you will be to handle the ups and downs of raising a puppy. Hopefully, everyone in the household is willing to do his part in raising and caring for the pup. The anticipation of owning a dog often brings a lot of promises from excited family members: "I will walk him every day," "I will feed him," "I will house-train him," etc., but these things take time and effort, and promises can easily be forgotten once the novelty of the new pet has worn off.

PET INSURANCE

Just like you can insure your car, your house and your own health, you likewise can insure your dog's health. Investigate a pet insurance policy by talking to your vet. Depending on the age of your dog, the breed and the kind of coverage you desire, your policy can be very affordable. Most policies cover accidental injuries, poisoning and thousands of medical problems and illnesses, including cancers. Some carriers also offer routine care and immunization coverage.

that it may not be readily discernible from a distance, although it is easily felt when the pup is held. The trembling can remain constant or it can be progressive, with some dogs becoming affected later or more seriously than is typical.

Thus far, this condition exists only in the UK. The disease has been traced to a Bernese named Duntiblae Nalle, a Swedish import who is the apparent common ancestor and first known carrier. Carriers can be identified only when bred to another carrier and affected puppies are produced. Carriers are normal, unaffected dogs, showing no signs of carrying the bad gene, and thus many carriers are unrecognized. It is known that carrier dogs have been exported to other countries, which could introduce the problem elsewhere. Outcrossing Nalle descendants will prevent producing affected pups, but can still produce carriers. The responsibility lies heavily on the breeders' shoulders.

COMMITMENT OF OWNERSHIP
After considering all of these factors, you have most likely already made some very important decisions about selecting your puppy. You have chosen a Bernese Mountain Dog, which means that you have decided which characteristics you want in a dog and what type of dog will best fit into your family and lifestyle. If you have selected a breeder, you have gone a step further—you have done your research and found a responsible, conscientious person who breeds quality Bernese and who should be a reliable source of help as you and your puppy adjust to life together. If you have observed a litter in action, you have obtained a firsthand look at the dynamics of a puppy "pack" and, thus, you should learn about each pup's individual personality—perhaps you have even found one that particularly appeals to you.

However, even if you have not yet found the Bernese puppy of your dreams, observing pups will help you learn to recognize certain behavior and to determine what a pup's behavior indicates

Puppies learn the "way of the world" from members of their pack. Littermates rough and tumble to learn what it is to "be dog."

about his temperament. You will be able to pick out which pups are the leaders, which ones are less outgoing, which ones are confident, which ones are shy, playful, aggressive, and so forth.

TIME TO GO HOME

Breeders rarely release puppies until they are eight to ten weeks of age. This is an acceptable age for most breeds of dog, excepting Toy breeds, which are not released until around 12 weeks, given their petite sizes. If a breeder has a puppy that is 12 weeks of age or older, he is likely well socialized and house-trained. Be sure that he is other-wise healthy before deciding to take him home.

Equally as important, you will learn to recognize what a healthy pup should look and act like. All of these things will help you in your search, and when you find the Berner that was meant for you, you will know it!

Researching your breed, selecting a responsible breeder and observing as many pups as possible are all important steps on the way to dog ownership. It may seem like a lot of effort…and you have not even taken the pup home yet! Remember, though, you cannot be too careful when it comes to deciding on the type of dog you want and finding out about your prospective pup's background. Buying a puppy is not—or should not be—just another whimsical purchase. This is one instance in which you actually do get to choose your own family! You may be thinking that buying a puppy should be fun—it should not be so serious and so much work. Keep in mind that your puppy is not a cuddly stuffed toy or decorative lawn ornament, but a creature that will become a real member of your family. You will come to realize that, while buying a puppy is a pleasurable and exciting endeavor, it is not something to be taken lightly. Relax...the fun will start when the pup comes home!

Always keep in mind that a puppy is nothing more than a baby in a furry disguise...a baby who is virtually helpless in a human world and who trusts his owner for fulfillment of his basic needs for survival. In addition to food, water and shelter, your pup needs care, protection, guidance and love. If you are not prepared to commit to this, then you are not prepared to own a dog.

"Wait a minute," you say. "How hard could this be? All of my neighbors own dogs and they seem to be doing just fine. Why should I have to worry about all of this?" Well, you should not worry about it; in fact, you will probably find that once your Bernese pup gets used to his new home, he will fall into his place in the family quite naturally. But it never hurts to emphasize the commitment of dog ownership. With some time and patience, it is really not too difficult to raise a curious and exuberant Bernese pup to be a well-adjusted and well-mannered adult dog—a dog that could be your most loyal friend.

PREPARING PUPPY'S PLACE IN YOUR HOME

Researching your breed and finding a breeder are only two aspects of the "homework" you will have to do before taking your Bernese puppy home. You will also have to prepare your home and family for the new addition. Much as you would prepare a nursery for a newborn baby, you will need to designate a place in your home that will be the puppy's own. How you prepare your home will depend on how much freedom the dog will be allowed. Whatever you decide, you must insure that he has a place that he can "call his own."

When you bring your new puppy into your home, you are

ARE YOU A FIT OWNER?
If the breeder from whom you are buying a puppy asks you a lot of personal questions, do not be insulted. Such a breeder wants to be sure that you will be a fit provider for his puppy.

bringing him into what will become his home as well. Obviously, you did not buy a puppy so that he could take over your house, but in order for a puppy to grow into a stable, well-adjusted dog, he has to feel comfortable in his surroundings. Remember, he is leaving the warmth and security of his mother and littermates, as well as the familiarity of the only place he has ever known, so it is important to make his transition as easy as possible. By preparing a place in your home for the puppy, you are making him feel as welcome as possible in a strange new place. It should not take him long to get used to it, but the sudden shock of being transplanted is somewhat traumatic for a young pup. Imagine how a small child would feel in the same situation—that is how your puppy must be feeling. It is up to you to reassure him and to let him know, "Little *hund*, you are going to like it here!"

WHAT YOU SHOULD BUY

CRATE

To someone unfamiliar with the use of crates in dog training, it may seem like punishment to shut a dog in a crate, but this is not the case at all. Most breeders and trainers recommend crates as preferred tools for show puppies as well as pet puppies. Crates are not cruel—crates have many

YOUR SCHEDULE...
If you lead an erratic, unpredictable life, with daily or weekly changes in your work requirements, consider the problems of owning a puppy. The new puppy has to be fed regularly, socialized (loved, petted, handled, introduced to other people) and, most importantly, allowed to go outdoors for house-training. As the dog gets older, he can be more tolerant of deviations in his feeding and relief schedule.

humane and highly effective uses in dog care and training. For example, crate training is a very popular and very successful house-training method. A crate can keep your dog safe during travel and, perhaps most importantly, a crate provides your dog with a place of his own in your home. It serves as a "doggie bedroom" of sorts—your Bernese

Photo courtesy of Doskocil

Crates of various sizes are available at your local pet shop. Purchase a crate large enough for a full-grown Berner.

something a little more luxurious than what his early ancestors enjoyed.

As far as purchasing a crate, the type that you buy is up to you. It will most likely be one of the two most popular types: wire or fiberglass. There are advantages and disadvantages to each type. For example, a wire crate is more open, allowing the air to flow through and affording the dog a view of what is going on around him, while a fiberglass crate is sturdier. Both can double as travel crates, providing protection for the dog. The size of the crate is another thing to consider. Puppies do not stay puppies forever—in fact, sometimes it seems as if they grow right before your eyes. A small crate may be fine for a very young Bernese pup, but it will not do him much good for long! Unless you have the money and the inclination to buy a new crate every time your pup has a growth spurt, it is better to get one that will accommodate your dog both as a pup and at full size. At 75 to 100 pounds as an adult, your Berner will require and extra-large crate, 24–26 inches wide and 38–52 inches long.

BEDDING
A soft mat in the dog's crate will help the dog feel more at home and you may also like to give him a small blanket. This will take the place of the leaves, twigs, etc.,

can curl up in his crate when he wants to sleep or when he just needs a break. Many dogs sleep in their crates overnight. With soft bedding and his favorite toy, a crate becomes a cozy pseudo-den for your dog. Like his ancestors, he too will seek out the comfort and retreat of a den—you just happen to be providing him with

that the pup would use in the wild to make a den; the pup can make his own "burrow" in the crate. Although your pup is far removed from his den-making ancestors, the denning instinct is still a part of his genetic makeup. Second, until you take your pup home, he has been sleeping amid the warmth of his mother and littermates, and while a blanket is not the same as a warm, breathing body, it still provides heat and something with which to snuggle. You will want to wash your pup's bedding frequently in case he has an "accident" in his crate, and replace or remove any blanket that becomes ragged and starts to fall apart.

Toys

Toys are a must for dogs of all ages, especially for curious playful pups. Puppies are the "children" of the dog world, and what child does not love toys? Chew toys provide enjoyment for both dog and owner—your dog will enjoy playing with his favorite toys, while you will enjoy the fact that they distract him from your expensive shoes and leather sofa. Puppies love to chew; in fact, chewing is a physical need for pups as they are teething, and everything looks appetizing! The full range of your possessions— from new boots to Oriental carpet—are fair game in the eyes of a teething pup. Puppies are not

CRATE-TRAINING TIPS

During crate training, you should partition off the section of the crate in which the pup stays. If he is given too big an area, this will hinder your training efforts. Crate training is based on the fact that a dog does not like to soil his sleeping quarters, so it is ineffective to keep a pup in an area that is so big that he can eliminate in one end and get far enough away from it to sleep. Also, you want to make the crate den-like for the pup. Blankets and a favorite toy will make the crate cozy for the small pup; as he grows, you may want to evict some of his "roommates" to make more room. It will take some coaxing at first, but be patient. Given some time to get used to it, your pup will adapt to his new home-within-a-home quite nicely.

TOYS, TOYS, TOYS!

With a big variety of dog toys available, and so many that look like they would be a lot of fun for a dog, be careful in your selection. It is amazing what a set of puppy teeth can do to an innocent-looking toy, so, obviously, safety is a major consideration. Be sure to choose the most durable products that you can find. Hard nylon bones and toys are a safe bet, and many of them are offered in different scents and flavors that will be sure to capture your dog's attention. It is always fun to play a game of fetch with your dog, and there are balls and flying discs that are specially made to withstand dog teeth.

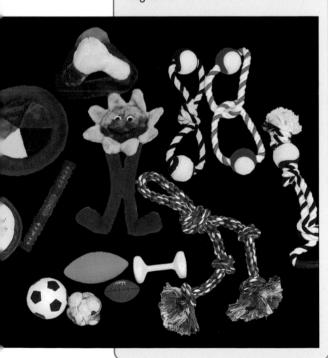

all that discerning when it comes to finding something to literally "sink their teeth into"—everything tastes great!

Bernese puppies are fairly active chewers and only the safest toys should be offered to them. Breeders advise owners to resist stuffed toys, because they can become de-stuffed in no time. The overly excited pup may ingest the stuffing, which can cause stomach problems.

Similarly, squeaky toys are quite popular, but must be avoided for the Bernese. Perhaps a squeaky toy can be used as an aid in training, but not for free play. If a pup "disembowels" one of these, the small plastic squeaker inside can be dangerous if swallowed. Monitor the condition of all of your pup's toys carefully and get rid of any that have been chewed to the point of becoming potentially dangerous.

Be careful of natural bones, which have a tendency to splinter into sharp, dangerous pieces. Also be careful of rawhide, which can turn into pieces that are easy to swallow and become a mushy mess on your carpet.

LEAD

A nylon lead is probably the best option as it is the most resistant to puppy teeth, should your pup take a liking to chewing on his lead. Of course, this is a habit that should be nipped in the bud, but if your

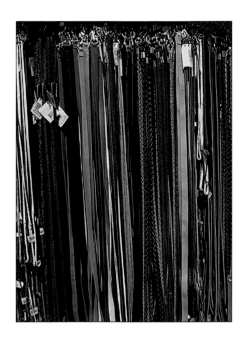

pup likes to chew on his lead he has a very slim chance of being able to chew through the strong nylon. Nylon leads are also light-weight, which is good for a young Bernese who is just getting used to the idea of walking on a lead.

Your local pet shop will surely have a large array of leads from which you can select the leads which best suit your needs. The training lead will usually differ from the lead used when the dog is fully trained to heel.

MENTAL AND DENTAL

Toys not only help your puppy get the physical and mental stimulation he needs but also provide a great way to keep his teeth clean. Hard rubber or nylon toys, especially those constructed with grooves, are designed to scrape away plaque, preventing bad breath and gum infection.

For everyday walking and safety purposes, the nylon lead is a good choice. As your pup grows up and gets used to walking on the lead, you may want to purchase a flexible lead. These leads allow you to extend the length to give the dog a broader area to explore or to shorten the length to keep the dog near you. Of course there are special leads for training purposes, and specially made leather harnesses,

Puppies like soft toys for chewing. Because they are teething, soft items like stuffed toys soothe their aching gums.

Your local pet shop will have a large selection of dog bowls from which you can make a selection. You should have separate water and food bowls for inside and out.

for carting activities, but these are not necessary for routine walks.

COLLAR

Your pup should get used to wearing a collar all of the time since you will want to attach his ID tags to it, plus you have to attach the lead to something! A lightweight nylon collar is a good choice; make sure that it fits snugly enough so that the pup cannot wriggle out of it, but is loose enough so that it will not be uncomfortably tight around the pup's neck. You should be able to fit a finger or two between the pup and the collar. It may take some time for your pup to get used to wearing the collar, but soon he will not even notice that it is there. Choke collars are made for training, but should only be used by an experienced handler.

THE RIDE HOME

Taking your dog from the breeder to your home in a car can be a very uncomfortable experience for both of you. The puppy will have been taken from his warm, friendly, safe environment and brought into a strange new environment—an environment that moves! Be prepared for loose bowels, urination, crying, whining and even fear biting. With proper love and encouragement when you arrive home, the stress of the trip should quickly disappear.

CHOOSE AN APPROPRIATE COLLAR

The **BUCKLE COLLAR** is the standard collar used for everyday purposes. Be sure that you adjust the buckle on growing puppies. Check it every day. It can become too tight overnight! These collars can be made of leather or nylon. Attach your dog's identification tags to this collar.

The **CHOKE COLLAR** is designed for training. It is constructed of highly polished steel so that it slides easily through the stainless steel loop. The idea is that the dog controls the pressure around his neck and he will stop pulling if the collar becomes uncomfortable.

The **HALTER** is for a trained dog that has to be restrained to prevent running away, chasing a cat and the like. Considered the most humane of all collars, it is frequently used on smaller dogs on which collars are not comfortable.

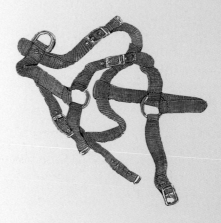

It is the owner's responsibility to pick up after his Bernese Mountain Dog has relieved himself.

FOOD AND WATER BOWLS

Your pup will need two bowls, one for food and one for water. You may want two sets of bowls, one for inside and one for outside, depending on where the dog will be fed and where he will be spending time. Stainless steel or sturdy plastic bowls are popular choices. Plastic bowls are more chewable. Dogs tend not to chew on the steel variety, which can be sterilized. It is important to buy sturdy bowls since anything is in danger of being chewed by puppy teeth and you do not want your dog to be constantly chewing apart his bowl (for his safety and for your purse!).

CLEANING SUPPLIES

Until a pup is house-trained, you will be doing a lot of cleaning. Accidents will occur, which is acceptable in the beginning because the puppy does not know any better. All you can do is be prepared to clean up any accidents. Old rags, towels, newspapers and a safe disinfectant are good to have on hand.

BEYOND THE BASICS

The items previously discussed are the bare necessities. You will find out what else you need as you go along—grooming supplies, flea/tick protection, baby gates to partition a room, etc. These things will vary depending on your situation but it is important that you have everything you need to feed and make your Bernese comfortable in his first few days at home.

FINANCIAL RESPONSIBILITY

Grooming tools, collars, leashes, crate, dog beds and, of course, toys will be expenses to you when you first obtain your pup, and the cost will continue throughout your dog's lifetime. If your puppy damages or destroys your possessions (as most puppies surely will!) or something belonging to a neighbor, you can calculate additional expense. There is also flea and pest control, which every dog owner faces more than once. You must be able to handle the financial responsibility of owning a dog.

PUPPY-PROOFING YOUR HOME

Aside from making sure that your Bernese will be comfortable in your home, you also have to make sure that your home is safe for your Bernese. This means taking precautions that your pup will not get into anything he should not get into and that there is nothing within his reach that may harm him should he sniff it, chew it, inspect it, etc. This probably seems obvious since, while you are primarily concerned with your pup's safety, at the same time you do not want your belongings to be ruined. Breakables should be placed out of reach if your dog is to have full run of the house. If he is to be limited to certain places within the house, keep any potentially dangerous items in the "off-limits" areas. An electrical cord can pose a danger should the puppy decide to taste it—and who is going to convince a pup that it would not make a great chew toy? Cords should be fastened tightly against the wall. If your dog is going to spend time in a crate, make sure that there is nothing near his crate that he can reach if he sticks his curious little nose or paws through the openings. Just as you would with a child, keep all household cleaners and chemicals where the pup cannot reach them.

It is also important to make sure that the outside of your home is safe. Of course your puppy should never be unsupervised, but a pup let loose in the yard will want to run and explore, and he should be granted that freedom.

PLAY'S THE THING

Teaching the puppy to play with his toys in running and fetching games is an ideal way to help the puppy develop muscle, learn motor skills and bond with you, his owner and master. He also needs to learn how to inhibit his bite reflex and never to use his teeth on people, forbidden objects and other animals in play. Whenever you play with your puppy, you make the rules. This becomes an important message to your puppy in teaching him that you are the pack leader and control everything he does in life. Once your dog accepts you as his leader, your relationship with him will be cemented for life.

should have an appointment arranged for your pup before you pick him up.

The pup's first visit will consist of an overall examination to make sure that the pup does not have any problems that are not apparent to the owner. The veterinarian will also set up a schedule for the pup's vaccinations; the breeder will inform you of which ones the pup has already received and the vet can continue from there.

INTRODUCTION TO THE FAMILY

Everyone in the house will be excited about the puppy's coming

If you have acquired your Berner pup from a reputable breeder, you should have every confidence that your vet will give him a spotless bill of health.

Berners are not known for climbing fences or digging under them, although a bored Berner may dig holes out of frustration. A 5- to 6-foot fence, well-embedded into the ground, is recommended to keep your Bernese safe.

FIRST TRIP TO THE VET

You have selected your puppy, and your home and family are ready. Now all you have to do is collect your Berner from the breeder and the fun begins, right? Well…not so fast. Something else you need to prepare is your pup's first trip to the veterinarian. Perhaps the breeder can recommend someone in the area who specializes in large-breed dogs or maybe you know some other Bernese owners who can suggest a good vet. Either way, you

SKULL & CROSSBONES

Thoroughly puppy-proof your house before bringing your puppy home. Never use cockroach or rodent poisons or plant fertilizers in any area accessible to the puppy. Avoid the use of toilet cleaners. Most dogs are born with "toilet-bowl sonar" and will take a drink if the lid is left open. Also keep the trash secured and out of reach.

home and will want to pet him and play with him, but it is best to make the introduction low-key so as not to overwhelm the puppy. He is apprehensive already. It is the first time he has been separated from his mother and the breeder, and the ride to your home is likely to be the first time he has been in a car. The last thing you want to do is smother him, as this will only frighten him further. This is not to say that human contact is not extremely necessary at this stage, because this is the time when a connection between the pup and his human family is formed. Gentle petting and soothing words should help console him, as well as just putting him down and letting him explore on his own (under your watchful eye, of course).

Berner puppies are curious and active, ready to investigate every inch of your yard. Be on guard when your puppy is roaming about your grounds to make sure all is safe for his inspection.

HOME DANGERS

Examine your grass and garden landscaping before bringing your puppy home. Many varieties of plants have leaves, stems or flowers that are toxic if ingested, and you can depend on a curious puppy to investigate them.

Scour your garage for potential puppy dangers. Remove weed killers, pesticides and antifreeze materials. Antifreeze is highly toxic and even a few drops can kill a dog. The sweet taste attracts the animal, who will quickly consume it from the floor or curbside. Ask your vet for information on poisonous plants or research them at your library.

Provide your puppy with clean water whenever he is outdoors playing.

The pup may approach the family members or may busy himself with exploring for a while. Gradually, each person should spend some time with the pup, one at a time, crouching down to get as close to the pup's level as possible and letting him sniff their hands and petting him gently. He definitely needs human attention and he needs to be touched—this is how to form an immediate bond. Just remember that the pup is experiencing a lot of things for the first time, at the same time. There are new people, new noises, new smells and new things to investigate: so be gentle, be affectionate and be as comforting as you can be.

PUP'S FIRST NIGHT HOME

You have traveled home with your new charge safely in his crate. He's been to the vet for a thorough check-up; he's been weighed, his papers examined; perhaps he's even been vaccinated and wormed as well. He's met the family, licked the whole family, including the excited children and the less-than-happy cat. He's explored his area, his new bed, the yard and anywhere else he's been permitted. He's eaten his first meal at home and relieved himself in the proper place. He's heard lots of new sounds, smelled new friends and seen more of the outside world than ever before.

That was just the first day! He's worn out and is ready for bed…or so you think! It's puppy's first night and you are ready to say "Good night"—keep in mind that this is puppy's first night ever to be sleeping alone. His

Properly socialized, Berners will happily make the acquaintance of your house cat, particularly if your cat is smartly tri-colored like this delightful Swiss kitty.

dam and littermates are no longer at paw's length and he's a bit scared, cold and lonely. Be reassuring to your new family member. This is not the time to spoil him and give in to his inevitable whining.

Puppies whine. They whine to let others know where they are and hopefully to get company out of it. Place your pup in his new bed or crate in his room and close the door. Mercifully, he may fall asleep without a peep. When the inevitable occurs, ignore the whining: he is fine. Be strong and keep his interest in mind. Do not allow yourself to feel guilty and visit the pup. He will fall asleep eventually.

Many breeders recommend placing a piece of bedding from his former home in his new bed so that he recognizes the scent of his littermates. Others advise placing a hot water bottle in his bed for warmth. This latter may be a good idea provided the pup doesn't attempt to suckle—he'll get good and wet and may not fall asleep so fast.

Puppy's first night can be somewhat stressful for the pup and his new family. Remember that you are setting the tone of nighttime at your house. Unless you want to play with your pup every night at 10 p.m., midnight and 2 a.m., don't initiate the habit. Your family will thank you, and so will your pup!

IN DUE TIME
It will take at least two weeks for your puppy to become accustomed to his new surroundings. Give him lots of love, attention, handling, frequent opportunities to relieve himself, a diet he likes to eat and a place he can call his own.

PREVENTING PUPPY PROBLEMS

SOCIALIZATION
Now that you have done all of the preparatory work and have helped your pup get accustomed to his new home and family, it is about time for you to have some fun! Socializing your Bernese pup gives you the opportunity to show off your new friend, and your pup gets to reap the benefits of being an adorable furry creature that

people will want to pet and, in general, think is absolutely precious!

Besides getting to know his new family, your puppy should be exposed to other people, animals and situations, but he must not come into close contact with dogs you don't know well until his course of injections is fully complete. This will help him become well adjusted as he grows up and less prone to being timid or fearful of the new things he will encounter. Your pup's socialization began with the breeder but now it is your responsibility to continue it. The socialization he receives up until the age of 12 weeks is the most critical, as this is the time when he forms his impressions of the outside world. Be especially careful during the eight-to-ten-week period, also known as the fear period. The interaction he receives during this time should be gentle and reassuring. Lack of socialization can manifest itself in fear and aggression as the dog grows up. He needs lots of human contact, affection, handling and exposure to other animals.

Once your pup has received his necessary vaccinations, feel free to take him out and about (on his lead, of course). Walk him around the neighborhood,

Socialization of your Berner as a puppy will insure good behavior as an adult. Dogs that have not been socialized properly can become overly shy or aggressive with other dogs.

take him on your daily errands, let people pet him, let him meet other dogs and pets, etc. Puppies do not have to try to make friends; there will be no shortage of people who will want to intro-duce themselves. Just make sure that you carefully supervise each meeting. If the neighborhood children want to say hello, for example, that is great—children and pups most often make great companions. Sometimes an excited child can unintentionally handle a pup too roughly, or an overzealous pup can playfully nip a little too hard. You want to make socialization experiences positive ones. What a pup learns

PUP MEETS WORLD
Thorough socialization includes not only meeting new people but also being introduced to new experiences such as riding in the car, having his coat brushed, hearing the television, walking in a crowd—the list is endless. The more your pup experiences, and the more positive the experiences are, the less of a shock and the less frightening it will be for your pup to encounter new things.

during this very formative stage will affect his attitude toward future encounters. You want your dog to be comfortable

All puppies welcome structure in their world. Place gates between rooms to indicate the "off-limits" zone of the house. Your Berner will accept whatever rules you fairly enforce.

SOCIALIZATION PERIOD

The socialization period for puppies is from age 8 to 16 weeks. This is the time when puppies need to leave their birth family and take up residence with their new owners, where they will meet many new people, other pets, etc. Failure to be adequately socialized can cause the dog to grow up fearing others and being shy and unfriendly due to a lack of self-confidence.

Be sure you have your puppy's attention before giving a command. Nothing is more pressing to a puppy than an itch!

for dominance, coupled with the fact that it is nearly impossible to look at an adorable Bernese pup with his fuzzy face and "puppy-dog" eyes and not cave in, give the pup almost an unfair advantage in getting the upper hand! A pup will definitely test the waters to see what he can and cannot do. Do not give in to those pleading eyes—stand your ground when it comes to disciplining the pup and make sure that all family members do the same. It will only confuse the pup when Mother tells him to get off the sofa when he is used to sitting up there with Father to watch the nightly news. Avoid

around everyone. A pup that has a bad experience with a child may grow up to be a dog that is shy around or aggressive toward children.

CONSISTENCY IN TRAINING

Dogs, being pack animals, naturally need a leader, or else they try to establish dominance in their packs. When you welcome a dog into your family, the choice of who becomes the leader and who becomes the "pack" is entirely up to you! Your pup's intuitive quest

discrepancies by having all members of the household decide on the rules before the pup even comes home…and be consistent in enforcing them! Early training shapes the dog's personality, so you cannot be unclear in what you expect.

COMMON PUPPY PROBLEMS

The best way to prevent puppy problems is to be proactive in stopping an undesirable behavior as soon as it starts. The old saying "You can't teach an old dog new tricks" does not necessarily hold true, but it is true that it is much easier to discourage bad behavior in a young developing pup than to wait until the pup's bad behavior becomes the adult dog's bad habit. There are some problems that are especially prevalent in puppies as they develop.

NIPPING

As puppies start to teethe, they feel the need to sink their teeth into anything available…unfortunately that includes your fingers, arms, hair and toes. You may find this behavior cute for the first *five seconds*…until you feel just how sharp those puppy teeth are. This is something you want to discourage immediately and consistently with a firm "No!" (or whatever number of firm "Nos" it takes for him to understand that you mean business). Then replace your finger with an appropriate chew toy.

MANNERS MATTER
During the socialization process, a puppy should meet people, experience different environments and definitely be exposed to other canines. Through playing and interacting with other dogs, your puppy will learn lessons, ranging from controlling the pressure of his jaws by biting his littermates to the inner-workings of the canine pack that he will apply to his human relationships for the rest of his life. That is why removing a puppy from its litter too early (before eight weeks) can be detrimental to the pup's development.

While this behavior is merely annoying when the dog is young, it can become dangerous as your Bernese's adult teeth grow in and his jaws develop, and he continues to think it is okay to gnaw on human appendages. Your Bernese does not mean any harm with a friendly nip, but he also does not know his own strength.

CRYING/WHINING

Your pup will often cry, whine, whimper, howl or make some type of commotion when he is left alone. This is basically his way of calling out for attention to make sure that you know he is there and that you have not forgotten about him. He feels insecure when he is left alone, when you are out of the house and he is in his crate or when you are in another part of the house and he cannot see you. The noise he is making is an expression of the anxiety he feels at being alone, so he needs to be taught that being alone is okay. You are not actually training the dog to stop making

The Berner puppy makes an attentive student who quickly absorbs commands and exercises, when the trainer is confident and clear in her desires.

CHEWING TIPS

Chewing goes hand in hand with nipping in the sense that a teething puppy is always looking for a way to soothe his aching gums. In this case, instead of chewing on you, he may have taken a liking to your favorite shoe or something else that he should not be chewing. Again, realize that this is a normal canine behavior that does not need to be discouraged, only redirected. Your pup just needs to be taught what is acceptable to chew on and what is off-limits. Consistently tell him "No!" when you catch him chewing on something forbidden and give him a chew toy.

Conversely, praise him when you catch him chewing on something appropriate. In this way, you are discouraging the inappropriate behavior and reinforcing the desired behavior. The puppy's chewing should stop after his adult teeth have come in, but an adult dog continues to chew for various reasons—perhaps because he is bored, needs to relieve tension or just likes to chew. That is why it is important to redirect his chewing when he is still young.

noise, you are training him to feel comfortable when he is alone and thus removing the need for him to make the noise. This is where the

With patience, consistency and lots of loving care, your Berner adolescents will grow into well-behaved handsome adult dogs.

crate with cozy bedding and a toy comes in handy. You want to know that he is safe when you are not there to supervise, and you know that he will be safe in his crate rather than roaming freely about the house. In order for the pup to stay in his crate without making a fuss, he needs to be comfortable in his crate. On that note, it is extremely important that the crate is never used as a form of punishment, or the pup will have a negative association with the crate.

Accustom the pup to the crate in short, gradually increasing time intervals in which you put him in the crate, maybe with a treat, and stay in the room with him. If he cries or makes a fuss, do not go to him, but stay in his sight. Gradually he will realize that staying in his crate is okay without your help, and it will not be so traumatic for him when you are not around. You may want to leave the radio on softly when you leave the house; the sound of human voices may be comforting to him.

> **STRESS-FREE**
> Some experts in canine health advise that stress during a dog's early years of development can compromise and weaken his immune system, and may trigger the potential for a shortened life. They emphasize the need for happy and stress-free growing-up years.

DIETARY AND FEEDING CONSIDERATIONS

For years it was believed that large breeds of dog required high-powered diets to support their rapid growth rates. This is not so today. It is now known that diets high in calories, primarily from fat and protein, actually contribute to skeletal problems during the first year of heavy growth. Veterinary nutritionists today recommend a balanced food that contains reduced amounts of fat and protein, and warn against supplementation with calcium and other vitamins, which could upset the balance of the food.

Today the choices of food for your Bernese are many and varied. There are simply dozens of brands of food in all sorts of flavors and varieties, ranging from puppy diets to those for seniors. There are even hypoallergenic and low-calorie diets available. Because your Bernese's food has a bearing on coat, health and temperament, it is essential that the most suitable diet is selected for a Bernese of his age. It is fair to say, however, that even experienced owners can be perplexed by the enormous range of foods available. Only understanding what is best for your dog will help you reach an informed decision.

Dog foods are produced in three basic types: dry, semi-moist and canned. Dry foods are useful

STORING DOG FOOD

You must store your dry dog food carefully. Open packages of dog food quickly lose their vitamin value, usually within 90 days of being opened. Free-feeding devices are not recommended for puppies, but may be viable for adult dogs.

for the cost-conscious for overall they tend to be less expensive than semi-moist or canned. They also contain the least fat and the most preservatives. In general, canned foods are made up of 60–70% water, while semi-moist ones often contain so much sugar that they are perhaps the least preferred by owners, even though their dogs seem to like them.

When selecting your dog's diet, three stages of development must be considered: the puppy stage, the adult stage and the senior stage. Let's take a look at each of these.

PUPPY STAGE

Puppies instinctively want to suck milk from their mother's teats and a normal puppy will exhibit this behavior from just a few moments following birth. If puppies do not attempt to suckle within the first half-hour or so, they should be encouraged to do so by placing them on the nipples, having selected ones with plenty of milk. This early milk supply is important in providing colostrum to protect the puppies during the first eight to ten weeks of their lives. Although a mother's milk is much better than any milk formula, despite there being some excellent ones available, if the puppies do not feed, the breeder will have to feed them himself. For those with less experience, advice from a veterinarian is

Experts recommend feeding the Berner from a bowl stand to help ward off bloat, which could result from the dog's craning his neck while eating or drinking.

important so that not only the right quantity of milk is fed but that of correct quality, fed at suitably frequent intervals, usually every two hours during the first few days of life.

Puppies should be allowed to nurse from their mother for about the first six weeks, although from the third or fourth week the breeder should begin to introduce small portions of suitable solid food. Most breeders like to introduce alternate milk and meat meals initially, building up to weaning time.

Puppies are weaned by the time they are about eight weeks old. Breeders offer their puppies top-quality puppy food, and owners should continue using the same brand once the puppy comes to his new home.

Bernese pups should be fed a high-quality diet designed specifically for large-breed pups during their first year. Owners should follow the advice of their vets when selecting the best puppy food for their Berners. Selection of the most suitable, good-quality diet at this time is essential, for a puppy's fastest growth rate is during the first year of life. Breeders are usually able to offer advice in this regard and, although the frequency of meals will have been reduced over time, only when a young dog has reached the age of about 12 months should an adult diet be fed. Puppy and junior diets should be well balanced for the needs of your dog, so that except in certain circumstances additional vitamins, minerals and proteins will not be required.

By the time the puppies are seven or a maximum of eight weeks old, they should be fully weaned and fed solely on a proprietary puppy food. Unless a special condition warrants it,

GRAIN-BASED DIETS

Some less expensive dog foods are based on grains and other plant proteins. While these products may appear to be attractively priced, many breeders prefer a diet based on animal proteins and believe that they are more conducive to your dog's health. Many grain-based diets rely on soy protein, which may cause flatulence (passing gas).

There are many cases, however, when your dog might require a special diet. These special requirements should only be recommended by your veterinarian.

ADULT DIETS

Adult Berners should eat the same high-quality food, with adjusted levels of fat and protein according to each dog's individual activity level, metabolism and health condition. Great care should be taken to keep a Berner lean and well-muscled, as overweight dogs are more prone to joint disease and other health problems, which can affect the heart, kidneys and liver.

A dog is considered an adult when he has stopped growing, so in general the diet of a Bernese

Mountain Dog can be changed to an adult one at about 12 months of age. Again you should rely upon your vet, breeder or dietary specialist to recommend an acceptable maintenance diet. Major dog-food manufacturers specialize in this type of food, and it is merely necessary for you to select the one best suited to your dog's needs.

SENIOR DIETS

As dogs get older, their metabolism changes. The Berner should be considered a senior by around five to seven years of age, depending on the activity level of the dog. The older dog usually exercises less, moves more slowly and sleeps more. This change in lifestyle and physiological performance requires a change in diet. Since these changes take place slowly, they might not be recognizable. What is easily recognizable is weight gain. By continuing to feed your dog an adult-maintenance diet when he is slowing down metabolically, your dog will gain weight. Obesity in an older dog compounds the health problems that already accompany old age.

As your dog gets older, few of his organs function up to par. The kidneys slow down and the intestines become less efficient. These age-related factors are best handled with a change in diet and a change in feeding schedule

FOOD PREFERENCE

Selecting the best dry dog food is difficult. There is no majority consensus among veterinary scientists as to the value of nutrient analysis (protein, fat, fiber, moisture, ash, cholesterol, minerals, etc.). All agree that feeding trials are what matter most, but you also have to consider the individual dog. The dog's weight, age and activity level, and what pleases his taste, all must be considered. It is probably best to take the advice of your veterinarian. Every dog has individual dietary requirements, and should be fed accordingly.

If your dog is fed a good dry food, he does not require supplements of meat or vegetables. Dogs do appreciate a little variety in their diets, so you may choose to stay with the same brand but vary the flavor. Alternatively, you may wish to add a little flavored stock to give a difference to the taste.

Your Berner depends on you to keep his mind and paws busy. An active dog will be a happy, healthy companion for you for many years.

to give smaller portions that are more easily digested.

There is no single best diet for every older dog. While many dogs do well on light or senior

TIPPING THE SCALES

Good nutrition is vital to your dog's health, but many people end up over-feeding or giving unnecessary supplements. Here are some common doggie diet don'ts:

• Adding milk, yogurt and cheese to your dog's diet may seem like a good idea for coat and skin care, but dairy products are very fattening and can cause indigestion.

• Diets high in fat will not cause heart attacks in dogs but will certainly cause your dog to gain weight and are harmful to growing pups.

• Never assume your dog will simply stop eating once he doesn't need any more food.

diets, other dogs do better on puppy diets or special premium diets such as lamb and rice. Be sensitive to your senior Berner's diet and this will help control other problems that may arise with your old friend.

WATER

Just as your dog needs proper nutrition from his food, water is an essential "nutrient" as well. Water keeps the dog's body properly hydrated and promotes normal function of the body's systems. During house-training, it is necessary to keep an eye on how much water your Bernese is drinking, but once he is reliably trained he should have access to clean fresh water at all times, especially if you feed dry food. Make certain that the dog's water bowl is clean, and change the water often.

EXERCISE

Working breeds require more exercise than most other breeds, and the Bernese Mountain Dog is no exception. A sedentary lifestyle is as harmful to a dog as it is to a person. The Bernese, a large dog with a substantial frame, needs to be walked twice daily for considerable distances. Berner pups should not be given vigorous exercise during the first year of life. Swimming is ideal for Berner pups. Keep the pup's daily walks short. Adults need free-running time as well to keep themselves fit. If you live in a home without a large fenced yard, you will have to commit to walking the dog for a few miles each day. For those who are more ambitious, you will find that your Bernese also enjoys an occasional hike, games of fetch or even a swim!

Bear in mind that an over-weight dog should never be suddenly over-exercised; instead he should be encouraged to increase exercise slowly. Not only is exercise essential to keep the dog's body fit, it is essential to his mental well-being. A bored dog will find something to do, which often manifests itself in some type of destructive behavior. In this sense, exercise is essential for the owner's mental well-being as well!

GROOMING

The Berner's coat is healthiest if brushed twice weekly. Regular

FEEDING TIPS

- Dog food must be served at room temperature, neither too hot nor too cold. Fresh water, changed often and served in a clean bowl, is mandatory, especially when feeding dry food.
- Never feed your dog from the table while you are eating, and never feed your dog leftovers from your own meal. They usually contain too much fat and too much seasoning.
- Dogs must chew their food. Hard pellets are excellent; soups and stews are to be avoided.
- Don't add leftovers or any extras to commercial dog food. The normal food is usually balanced, and adding something extra destroys the balance.
- Except for age-related changes, dogs do not require dietary variations. They can be fed the same diet, day after day, without their becoming bored or ill.

"DOES THIS COLLAR MAKE ME LOOK FAT?"

While humans may obsess about how they look and how trim their bodies are, many people believe that extra weight on their dogs is a good thing. The truth is, pets should not be over- or under-weight, as both can lead to or signal sickness. In order to tell how fit your pet is, run your hands over his ribs. Are his ribs buried under a layer of fat or are they sticking out considerably? If your pet is within his normal weight range, you should be able to feel the ribs easily, but they should not protrude abnormally. If you stand above him, the outline of his body should resemble an hourglass. Some breeds do tend to be leaner while some are a bit stockier, but making sure your dog is the right weight for his breed will certainly contribute to his good health.

frequent grooming is very beneficial to the dog's skin as well as the coat, as brushing massages the skin and distributes the natural oils throughout the coat, while also dispensing dirt and dust. Grooming a Bernese is not complicated or difficult. Basic tools include a coarse steel comb, a flea comb with closely spaced teeth and a slicker brush.

Start by brushing the long outer coat with the metal comb and loosen any snarls, then follow with your fine-toothed flea comb. Remove any loose hair with the slicker brush, brushing first against the grain, then with the grain for sheen. A damp chamois cloth is also handy for removing loose hair and dust.

Grooming, of course, also involves tending to the ears, eyes, teeth, feet and nails. A thorough body examination during grooming will disclose any lumps, sores or minor injuries or problems that may be hidden under the dense coat.

A well-kept Bernese should not require frequent bathing unless he gets into something smelly. Monthly baths are recommended, and a dry or waterless shampoo will spot-clean problem areas in between. Most Bernese shed about twice a year, and during those periods more frequent, even daily, brushing, will keep dog hair around the home to a minimum. Frequent bathing during shedding season will also help speed up the shedding process.

BATHING

Like most anything, if you accustom your Berner to being bathed as a puppy, it will be second nature by the time he grows up. You want your dog to be at ease in the bath or else it could end up a wet, soapy, messy ordeal for both of you!

Brush your Bernese thoroughly before wetting his coat. This will get rid of most mats and tangles, which are harder to remove when the coat is wet. Make certain that your dog has a good non-slip surface to stand

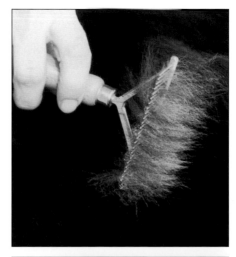

The Berner is a double-coated dog that will cast his coat twice per year, pushing out his soft undercoat. Purchase a top-quality rake or slicker brush to help remove the dead undercoat during grooming sessions.

GROOMING EQUIPMENT

Always purchase the best quality grooming equipment so that your tools will last for many years to come. Here are some basics:

- Slicker brush
- Chamois
- Flea comb
- Metal comb
- Scissors
- Rubber mat
- Dog shampoo
- Spray hose attachment
- Towels
- Blow dryer
- Ear cleaner
- Cotton balls
- Nail clippers
- Dental-care products

The Berner's coat benefits from two weekly brushing sessions. Such a regimen keeps shedding to a minimum.

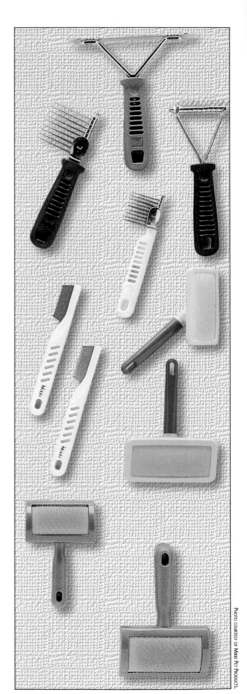

on. Begin by wetting the dog's coat. A shower or hose attachment is necessary for thoroughly wetting and rinsing the coat. Check the water temperature to make sure that it is neither too hot nor too cold.

Next, apply shampoo to the dog's coat and work it into a good lather. You should purchase a shampoo that is made for dogs. Do not use a product made for human hair. Wash the head last; you do not want shampoo to drip into the dog's eyes while you are washing the rest of his body. Work the shampoo all the way down to the skin. You can use this as another opportunity to check the skin for any bumps, bites or other abnormalties. Do not neglect any area of the body—get all of the hard-to-reach places.

Your local pet shop will have an adequate supply of grooming tools from which you can select those tools most appropriate for the task.

Once the dog has been thoroughly shampooed, he requires an equally thorough rinsing.

Shampoo left in the coat can be irritating to the skin. Protect his eyes from the shampoo by shielding them with your hand and directing the flow of water in the opposite direction. You should also avoid getting water in the ear canal. Be prepared for your dog to shake out his coat—you might want to stand back, but make sure you have a hold on the dog to keep him from running through the house.

TOOTH CARE

Just as you must brush your teeth every day, your Bernese Mountain Dog's teeth require regular care as well. Plaque and calculus buildup on your dog's teeth can lead to many serious health disorders, so

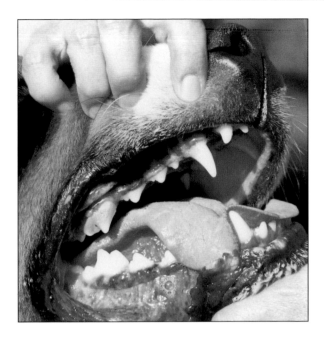

> **BATHING BEAUTY**
>
> Once you are sure that the dog is thoroughly rinsed, squeeze the excess water out of his coat with your hand and dry him with an heavy towel. You may choose to use a blow dryer on his coat or just let it dry naturally. In cold weather, never allow your dog outside with a wet coat.
>
> There are "dry bath" products on the market, which are sprays and powders intended for spot cleaning, that can be used between regular baths if necessary. They are not substitutes for regular baths, but they are easy to use for touch-ups as they do not require rinsing.

dental care is not merely a matter of shiny whites and minty breath. Of course, human dental products are not recommended for use on dogs as they can destroy the enamel on the dog's teeth. Pet shops sell dental-care products, including doggy toothbrushes, cleaning devices and toothpaste, which make the task easy. You should brush your dog's teeth once a week at the very least. Doggy toothpastes have appealing flavors (like liver or chicken) that will make the regimen "more palatable" for the puppy (or adult). Discuss tooth care with your veterinarian, and schedule a tooth scaling once a year. Just as you would visit your dentist annually for a cleaning, your dog

Owners must pay attention to their Berner's dentition. Brushing and checking for tooth decay are important parts of maintaining your dog's health.

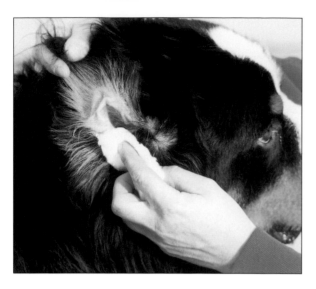

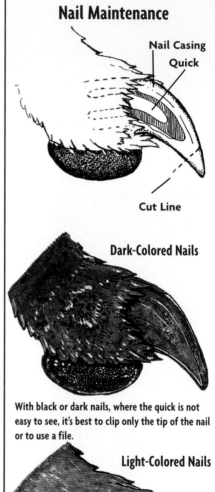

Nail Maintenance

Nail Casing

Quick

Cut Line

Dark-Colored Nails

With black or dark nails, where the quick is not easy to see, it's best to clip only the tip of the nail or to use a file.

Light-Colored Nails

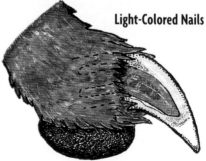

In light-colored nails, clipping is much simpler because you can see the vein (or quick) that grows inside the casing.

Your Berner's ears should be cleaned as frequently as your dog is groomed. Use soft cotton balls with ear powder made especially for dogs.

should visit the vet to clean his teeth. Smile and enjoy your Berner's gleaming pearly whites!

EAR CLEANING

The ears should be kept clean with a cotton ball and ear powder made especially for dogs. Be on the lookout for any signs of infection or ear-mite infestation. If your Bernese has been shaking his head or scratching at his ears frequently, this usually indicates a problem. If his ears have an unusual odor, this is a sure sign of mite infestation or infection, and a signal to have his ears checked by the veterinarian.

NAIL CLIPPING

Your Bernese should be accustomed to having his nails trimmed at an early age, since it

will be a part of your maintenance routine throughout his life. Not only does it look nicer, but long nails can scratch someone unintentionally. Also, a long nail has a better chance of ripping and bleeding, or causing the feet to spread. A good rule of thumb is that if you can hear your dogs' nails clicking on the floor when he walks, his nails are too long.

Before you start cutting, make sure you can identify the "quick" in each nail. The quick is a blood vessel that runs through the center of each nail and grows rather close to the end. It will bleed if accidentally cut, which will be quite painful for the dog as it contains nerve endings. Keep some type of clotting agent on hand, such as a styptic pencil or styptic powder (the type used for shaving). This will stop the bleeding quickly when applied to the end of the cut nail. Do not panic if you cut the quick, just stop the bleeding and talk soothingly to your dog. Once he has calmed down, move on to the next nail. It is better to clip a little at a time, particularly with black-nailed dogs.

The time and effort that you invest in your Berner's diet, coat care and exercise pay off in your having a handsome companion dog who is a pleasure to have around.

Hold your pup steady as you begin trimming his nails; you do not want him to make any sudden movements or run away. Talk to him soothingly and stroke him as you clip. Holding his foot in your hand, simply take off the end of each nail in one quick clip. You can purchase nail clippers that are specially made for dogs; you can probably find them wherever you buy pet or grooming supplies.

TRAVELING WITH YOUR DOG

CAR TRAVEL

You should accustom your Bernese to riding in a car at an early age. You may or may not take him in the car often, but at the very least he will need to go to the vet and you do not want these trips to be traumatic for the dog or troublesome for you. The safest way for a dog to ride in the car is in his crate. If he uses a crate in the house, you can use the same crate for travel, provided your vehicle can accommodate such a large crate.

Put the pup in the crate and see how he reacts. If he seems uneasy, you can have a passenger hold him on his lap while you drive. Another option is a specially made safety harness for dogs, which straps the pup in much like a seat belt. Do not let the dog roam loose in the vehicle—this is very dangerous! If you should stop

short, your dog can be thrown and injured. If the dog starts climbing on you and pestering you while you are driving, you will not be able to concentrate on the road. It is an unsafe situation for everyone—human and canine.

LET THE SUN SHINE
Your dog needs daily sunshine for the same reason people do. Pets kept inside homes with curtains drawn against the sun suffer from "SAD" (Seasonal Affected Disorder) to the same degree as humans. We now know that sunlight must enter the iris and thus to the pineal gland to regulate the body's hormonal system and when we live and work in artificial light, both circadian rhythms and hormone balances are disturbed.

Owners of large dogs like Bernese Mountain Dogs ideally have vehicles that can accommodate their full-sized dogs. A van, station wagon or a sports utility vehicle would serve the needs of a devoted Berner owner and his dog better than a sports car or similar smaller car. The dog's crate can easily fit into a van or a large SUV, though a partition in a station wagon or similar vehicle can keep your Berner toward the rear of the vehicle away from the driver. Your safety depends on properly confining the dog while you are traveling.

For long trips, be prepared to stop to let the dog relieve himself. Take with you water and a bowl along with whatever you

The only safe way to travel with a Berner in the car or van is in his crate or behind a divider, which keeps the dog from disturbing the driver (and other passengers) while travelling.

need to clean up after him, including some paper towels for use should he have an accident in the car or suffer from motion sickness.

AIR TRAVEL

Contact your chosen airline before proceeding with your travel plans that include your Bernese Mountain Dog. The dog will be required to travel in a fiberglass crate and you should always check in advance with the airline regarding specific requirements. To help put the dog at ease, give him one of his favorite toys in the crate. Do not feed the dog for at least six hours before the trip in order to minimize his need to relieve himself. However, certain regulations specify that water must always be made available to the dog in the crate. Make sure your dog is properly identified and that your contact information appears on his ID tags and on his crate.

VACATIONS AND BOARDING

So you want to take a family vacation—and you want to include *all* members of the family. You would probably make arrangements for accommodations ahead of time anyway, but this is especially important when traveling with a dog. You do not want to make an overnight stop at the only place around for miles and find out that they do

ON THE ROAD

If you are going on a long motor trip with your dog, be sure the hotels are dog-friendly. Many hotels do not accept dogs. Also take along some ice that can be thawed and offered to your dog if he becomes overheated. Most dogs like to lick ice.

not allow dogs. Also, you do not want to reserve a place for your family without confirming that you are traveling with a dog because, if it is against their policy, you may not have a place to stay.

Alternatively, if you are traveling and choose not to bring your Bernese, you will have to make arrangements for him while you are away. Some options are to take him to a neighbor's house to stay while you are gone, to have a trusted friend stop by often or stay at your house or to bring your dog to a reputable boarding kennel. If you choose to board him at a kennel, you should visit in advance to see the facilities provided, how clean they are and where the dogs are kept. Talk to some of the employees and see how they treat the dogs—do they spend time with the dogs, play with them, exercise them, etc.? Also find out the kennel's policy on vaccinations and what they require. This is for

If you acquire your Berner from a local breeder, you might be fortunate enough to board the dog with the breeder when you are on vacation. Otherwise, you will have to seek out a reputable facility near your home.

all of the dogs' safety, since when dogs are kept together, there is a greater risk of diseases being passed from dog to dog.

IDENTIFICATION

Your Berner is your valued companion and friend. That is why you always keep a close eye on him and you have made sure that he cannot escape from the yard or wriggle out of his collar and run away from you. However, accidents can happen and there may come a time when your dog unexpectedly gets separated from you. If this unfortunate event should occur, the first thing on your mind will be finding him. Proper identification, including an ID tag as well as a tattoo and/or a microchip, will increase the chances of his being returned to you safely and quickly.

As puppies become more and more expensive, especially those puppies of high quality for showing and/or breeding, they have a greater chance of being stolen. The usual collar dog tag is, of course, easily removed. But there are two more permanent techniques that have become widely used for identification.

The puppy microchip implantation involves the injection of a small microchip, about the size of a corn kernel, under the skin of the dog. If your dog shows up at a clinic or shelter, or is offered for resale under less-than-savory

circumstances, it can be positively identified by the microchip. The microchip is scanned, and a registry quickly identifies you as the owner.

Tattooing is done on various parts of the dog, from his belly to his ears. The number tattooed can be your telephone number, your dog's registration number or any other number that you can easily memorize. When professional dog thieves see a tattooed dog, they usually lose interest. For the safety of our dogs, no laboratory facility or dog broker will accept a tattooed dog as stock.

Discuss microchipping and tattooing with your veterinarian and breeder. Some vets perform these services on their own premises for a reasonable fee. To ensure that your dog's identification is effective, be certain that the dog is then properly registered with a legitimate national database.

Your Berner should always wear his identification tag attached to his everyday collar.

REAP THE REWARDS

If you start with a normal, healthy dog and give him time, patience and some carefully executed lessons, you will reap the rewards of that training for the life of the dog. And what a life it will be! The two of you will find immeasurable pleasure in the companionship you have built together with love, respect and understanding.

Living with an untrained dog is a lot like owning a piano that you do not know how to play—it is a nice object to look at but it does not do much more than that to bring you pleasure. Now try taking piano lessons and suddenly the piano comes alive and brings forth magical sounds and rhythms that set your heart singing and your body swaying.

The same is true with your Bernese Mountain Dog. Any dog is a big responsibility and if not trained sensibly may develop unacceptable behavior that annoys you or could even cause family friction.

To train your Berner, you may like to enroll him in an obedience class. Teach him good manners as you learn how and why he behaves the way he does. Find out how to communicate with your dog and how to recognize and understand his communications with you. Suddenly the dog takes on a new role in your life—he is clever, interesting, well-behaved and fun to be with. He demonstrates his bond of devotion to you daily. In other words, your Bernese does wonders for your

> ### THINK BEFORE YOU BARK
>
> Dogs are sensitive to their masters' moods and emotions. Use your voice wisely when communicating with your dog. Never raise your voice at your dog unless you are trying to correct him. "Barking" at your dog can become as meaningless as "dogspeak" is to you.

ego because he constantly reminds you that you are not only his leader, you are his hero!

Those involved with teaching dog obedience and counseling owners about their dogs' behavior have discovered some interesting facts about dog ownership. For example, training dogs when they are puppies results in the highest rate of success in developing well-mannered and well-adjusted adult dogs. Training an older dog, from six months to six years of age, can produce almost equal results providing that the owner accepts the dog's slower rate of learning capability and is willing to work patiently to help the dog succeed at developing to his fullest potential. Unfortunately, many owners of untrained adult dogs lack the patience factor, so they do not persist until their dogs are successful at learning particular behaviors.

Training a puppy aged 10 to 16 weeks (20 weeks at the most) is like working with a dry sponge in a pool of water. The pup soaks up whatever you show him and constantly looks for more things to do and learn. At this early age, his body is not yet producing hormones, and therein lies the reason for such a high rate of success. Without hormones, he is focused on his owners and not particularly interested in investigating other places, dogs, people, etc. You are his leader: his provider of food, water, shelter and security. He latches onto you and wants to stay close. He will usually follow you from room to room, will not let you out of his sight when you are outdoors with him and will respond in like manner to the people and animals you encounter. If you greet a friend warmly, he will be happy to greet the person as well. If, however, you are hesitant, even anxious, about the approach

Owners who invest the time and energy to train their dogs are immensely more content with their pets.

of a stranger, he will respond accordingly.

Once the puppy begins to produce hormones, his natural curiosity emerges and he begins to investigate the world around him. It is at this time when you may notice that the untrained dog begins to wander away from you and even ignore your commands to stay close. When this behavior becomes a problem, the owner has two choices: get rid of the dog or train him. It is

Your Berner puppy will stand on his hinds (or his head) for a tasty treat. Don't be afraid to bribe your Berner— bribery is no crime in the canine lexicon.

> **CALM DOWN**
> Dogs will do anything for your attention. If you reward the dog when he is calm and attentive, you will develop a well-mannered dog. If, on the other hand, you greet your dog excitedly and encourage him to wrestle with you, the dog will greet you the same way and you will have a hyperactive dog on your hands.

strongly urged that you choose the latter option.

There are usually classes within a reasonable distance from the owner's home, but you can also do a lot to train your dog yourself. Sometimes there are classes available but the tuition is too costly. Whatever the circumstances, the solution to training your Bernese without formal obedience classes lies within the pages of this book. This chapter is devoted to helping you train your Berner at home. If the recommended procedures are followed faithfully, you may expect positive results that will prove rewarding both to you and your dog.

Whether your new charge is a puppy or a mature adult, the methods of teaching and the techniques we use in training basic behaviors are the same. After all, no dog, whether puppy or adult, likes harsh or inhumane methods. All creatures, however, respond favorably to gentle motivational

methods and sincere praise and encouragement. Now let us get started.

HOUSE-TRAINING

You can train a puppy to relieve himself wherever you choose, but this must be somewhere suitable. You should bear in mind from the outset that when your puppy is old enough to go out in public places, any canine droppings must be removed at once. You will always have to carry with you a plastic bag or "poop-scoop."

Outdoor training includes such surfaces as grass, soil and cement. Indoor training usually means training your dog to newspaper. When deciding on the surface and location that you will want your Bernese to use, be sure it is going to be permanent. Training your dog to grass and then changing your mind two months later is extremely difficult for both dog and owner. Of course, outdoor training will be your choice for the Berner, although you may wish to reinforce the puppy's outdoor training with newspaper indoors temporarily.

Next, choose the command you will use each and every time you want your puppy to void. "Hurry up" and "Let's go" are examples of commands commonly used by dog owners.

Get in the habit of giving the puppy your chosen relief command before you take him out.

TAKE THE LEAD
Do not carry your dog to his relief area. Lead him there on a leash or, better yet, encourage him to follow you to the spot. If you start carrying him to his spot, you might end up doing this routine forever and your dog will have the satisfaction of having trained *you*.

That way, when he becomes an adult, you will be able to determine if he wants to go out when you ask him. A confirmation will be signs of interest—look for the puppy wagging his tail, watching you intently, going to the door, etc.

PUPPY'S NEEDS
The puppy needs to relieve himself after play periods, after

Toilet training, anyone? Remember what goes in must come out, so keep the amount of water your Berner puppy drinks in mind during house-training.

CANINE DEVELOPMENT SCHEDULE

It is important to understand how and at what age a puppy develops into adulthood.
If you are a puppy owner, consult the following Canine Development Schedule to
determine the stage of development your puppy is currently experiencing.
This knowledge will help you as you work with the puppy in the weeks and months ahead.

Period	Age	Characteristics
FIRST TO THIRD	BIRTH TO SEVEN WEEKS	Puppy needs food, sleep and warmth, and responds to simple and gentle touching. Needs mother for security and disciplining. Needs littermates for learning and interacting with other dogs. Pup learns to function within a pack and learns pack order of dominance. Begin socializing pup with adults and children for short periods. Pup begins to become aware of his environment.
FOURTH	EIGHT TO TWELVE WEEKS	Brain is fully developed. Pup needs socializing with outside world. Remove from mother and littermates. Needs to change from canine pack to human pack. Human dominance necessary. Fear period occurs between 8 and 12 weeks. Avoid fright and pain.
FIFTH	THIRTEEN TO SIXTEEN WEEKS	Training and formal obedience should begin. Less association with other dogs, more with people, places, situations. Period will pass easily if you remember this is pup's change-to-adolescence time. Be firm and fair. Flight instinct prominent. Permissiveness and over-disciplining can do permanent damage. Praise for good behavior.
JUVENILE	FOUR TO EIGHT MONTHS	Another fear period about 7 to 8 months of age. It passes quickly, but be cautious of fright and pain. Sexual maturity reached. Dominant traits established. Dog should understand sit, down, come and stay by now.

NOTE: THESE ARE APPROXIMATE TIME FRAMES. ALLOW FOR INDIVIDUAL DIFFERENCES IN PUPPIES.

PAPER CAPER

Never line your pup's sleeping area with newspaper. Puppy litters are usually raised on newspaper and, once in your home, the puppy will immediately associate newspaper with voiding. Never put newspaper on any floor while house-training, as this will only confuse the puppy. If you are paper-training him, use paper in his designated relief area only. Finally, restrict water intake after evening meals. Offer a few licks at a time—never let a young puppy gulp water after meals.

on the success of house-training, we consider the various aspects of both before we begin training.

Taking a new puppy home and turning him loose in your house can be compared to turning a child loose in a sports arena and telling the child that the place is all his! The sheer enormity of the place would be too much for him to handle.

Instead, offer the puppy clearly defined areas where he can play, sleep, eat and live. A room of the house where the family gathers is the most obvious choice. Puppies are social animals and need to feel a part of the pack right from the start. Hearing your voice, watching you while you are doing things and smelling you nearby are all positive reinforcers that he is now a

each meal, after he has been sleeping and at any time he indicates that he is looking for a place to urinate or defecate. The urinary and intestinal tract muscles of very young puppies are not fully developed. Therefore, like human babies, puppies need to relieve themselves frequently. Take your puppy out often—every hour for an eight-week-old, for example, and always immediately after sleeping and eating. The older the puppy, the less often he will need to relieve himself. Finally, as a mature healthy adult, he will require only three to five relief trips per day.

Housing
Since the types of housing and control you provide for your puppy have a direct relationship

Your puppy will welcome his crate as his own special place in no time. The crate is the best house-training method for Berners, and most breeders recommend the crate for reinforcing house-training.

member of your pack. Usually a family room, the kitchen or a nearby adjoining breakfast area is ideal for providing safety and security for both puppy and owner.

Within that room there should be a smaller area that the puppy can call his own. An alcove, a wire or fiberglass dog crate or a gated corner from which he can view the activities of his new family will be fine. The size of the area or crate is the key factor here. The area must be large enough for the puppy to lie down and stretch out as well as stand up without rubbing his head on the top, yet small enough so that he cannot relieve himself at one end and sleep at the other without coming into contact with his droppings until fully trained to relieve himself outside. The designated area should contain clean bedding and a toy. Water must always be available, in a non-spill container.

> **MEALTIME**
>
> Mealtime should be a peaceful time for your puppy. Do not put his food and water bowls in a high-traffic area in the house. For example, give him his own little corner of the kitchen where he can eat undisturbed and where he will not be underfoot. Do not allow small children or other family members to disturb the pup when he is eating.

Dogs are, by nature, clean animals and will not remain close to their relief areas unless forced to do so. In those cases, they then become dirty dogs and usually remain that way for life.

CONTROL

By *control*, we mean helping the puppy to create a lifestyle pattern that will be compatible to that of his human pack (*you!*). Just as we guide little children to learn our way of life, we must show the puppy when it is time to play, eat, sleep, exercise and even entertain himself.

Your puppy should always sleep in his crate. He should also learn that, during times of household confusion and excessive human activity such as at breakfast when family members are preparing for the day, he can play by himself in relative safety and comfort in his designated area. Each time you leave the puppy alone, he should understand exactly where he is to stay. Puppies are chewers. They cannot tell the difference between lamp cords, television wires, shoes, table legs, etc. Chewing into a television wire, for example, can be fatal to the puppy while a shorted wire can start a fire in the house.

If the puppy chews on the arm of the chair when he is alone, you will probably discipline him angrily when you get home. Thus, he makes the association that your coming home means he is going to be punished. (He will not remember chewing the chair and is incapable of making the association of the discipline with his naughty deed.)

Other times of excitement, such as family parties, holidays, etc., can be fun for the puppy providing he can view the activities from the security of his designated area. He is not underfoot and he is not being fed all sorts of tidbits that will probably cause him stomach distress, yet he still feels a part of the fun.

SCHEDULE

A puppy should be taken to his relief area each time he is released from his designated area, after meals, after a play session and when he first awakens in the morning (at age eight weeks, this can mean 5 a.m.!). The puppy will indicate that he's ready "to go" by circling or sniffing busily—do not misinterpret these signs. For a puppy less than ten weeks of age, a routine of taking him out every hour is necessary. As the puppy grows, he will be able to wait for longer periods of time.

Keep trips to his relief area short. Stay no more than five or six minutes and then return to the house. If he goes during that time, praise him lavishly and take him indoors immediately. If he does not, but he has an accident when you go back indoors, pick him up immediately, say "No! No!" and return to his relief area. Wait a few minutes, then return to the house again. Never hit a puppy or put his face in urine or excrement when he has had an accident! Such behavior

Never underestimate the power of the canine nose. Puppies remember every microcosm of scent, which can complicate house-training if you do not properly sanitize the area after an accident.

only makes the dog distrustful of his master.

Once indoors, put the puppy in his crate until you have had time to clean up his accident. Then release him to the family area and watch him more closely than before. Chances are, his accident was a result of your not picking up his signal or waiting too long before offering him the opportunity to relieve himself. Never hold a grudge against the puppy for accidents.

THE SUCCESS METHOD

Success that comes by luck is usually short-lived. Success that comes by well-thought-out proven methods is often more easily achieved and permanent. This is the Success Method. It is designed to give you, the puppy owner, a simple yet proven way to help your puppy develop clean living habits and a feeling of security in his new environment.

6 Steps to Successful Crate Training

1 Tell the puppy "Crate time!" and place him in the crate with a small treat (a piece of cheese or half of a biscuit). Let him stay in the crate for five minutes while you are in the same room. Then release him and praise lavishly. Never release him when he is fussing. Wait until he is quiet before you let him out.

2 Repeat Step 1 several times a day.

3 The next day, place the puppy in the crate as before. Let him stay there for ten minutes. Do this several times.

4 Continue building time in five-minute increments until the puppy stays in his crate for 30 minutes with you in the room. Always take him to his relief area after prolonged periods in his crate.

5 Now go back to Step 1 and let the puppy stay in his crate for five minutes, this time while you are out of the room.

6 Once again, build crate time in five-minute increments with you out of the room. When the puppy will stay willingly in his crate (he may even fall asleep!) for 30 minutes with you out of the room, he will be ready to stay in it for several hours at a time.

HOW MANY TIMES A DAY?

AGE	RELIEF TRIPS
To 14 weeks	10
14–22 weeks	8
22–32 weeks	6
Adulthood	4
(dog stops growing)	

These are estimates, of course, but
they are a guide to the minimum
number of opportunities a dog should
have each day to relieve himself.

Let the puppy learn that going
outdoors means it is time to
relieve himself, not play. Once
trained, he will be able to play
indoors and out and still differen-
tiate between the times for play
versus the times for relief.

Help him develop regular
hours for naps, being alone, playing by himself and just resting, all
in his crate. Encourage him to
entertain himself while you are
busy with your activities. Let him
learn that having you near is
comforting, but it is not your main
purpose in life to provide him
with undivided attention. Each
time you put a puppy in his own
area, use the same command,
whatever suits best. Soon he will
run to his crate or special area
when he hears you say those
words.

Crate training provides safety
for you, the puppy and the home.
It also provides the puppy with a
feeling of security, and that helps
the puppy achieve self-confidence
and clean habits. Remember that
one of the primary ingredients in

LANGUAGE BARRIER

Dogs do not understand our language and have to rely on tone of voice more than just words or sound. They can be trained to react to a certain sound, at a certain volume. If you say "No, Oliver" in a very soft, pleasant voice, it will not have the same meaning as "No, Oliver!!" when you raise your voice.

You should never use the dog's name during a reprimand, just the command "No! " You never want the dog to associate his name with a negative experience or reprimand.

house-training your puppy is control. Regardless of your lifestyle, there will always be occasions when you will need to have a place where your dog can stay and be happy and safe. Crate training is the answer for now and in the future.

In conclusion, a few key elements are really all you need for a successful house-training method—consistency, frequency, praise, control and supervision. By following these procedures with a normal, healthy puppy, you and the puppy will soon be past the stage of accidents and ready to move on to a tidy and rewarding life together.

ROLES OF DISCIPLINE, REWARD AND PUNISHMENT

Discipline, training one to act in accordance with rules, brings

Be fair and consistent when training your Berner. Few breeds are as sensitive to human emotions.

order to life. It is as simple as that. Without discipline, particularly in a group society, chaos reigns supreme and the group will eventually perish. Humans and canines are social animals and need some form of discipline in order to function effectively. They must procure food, reproduce to keep the species going and protect their home base and their young.

If there were no discipline in the lives of social animals, they would eventually die from starvation and/or predation by other stronger animals. In the case of domestic canines, dogs need discipline in their lives in order to understand how their pack (you and other family members) func-

tions and how they must act in order to survive.

A large humane society in a highly populated area recently surveyed dog owners regarding their satisfaction with their relationships with their dogs. People who had trained their dogs were 75% more satisfied with their pets than those who had never trained their dogs.

Dr. Edward Thorndike, a well-respected animal psychologist, established *Thorndike's Theory of Learning*, which states that a behavior that results in a pleasant event tends to be repeated. Thus, a behavior that results in an unpleasant event tends not to be repeated. It is this theory on which training methods are based today. For example, if you manipulate a dog to perform a specific behavior and reward him for doing it, he is likely to do it again because he enjoyed the end result.

Occasionally, punishment, a penalty inflicted for an offense, is necessary. The best type of punishment often comes from an outside source. For example, a child is told not to touch the stove because he may get burned. He disobeys and touches the stove. In doing so, he receives a burn. From that time on, he respects the heat of the stove and avoids contact with it. Therefore, a behavior that results in an unpleasant event tends not to be repeated.

KEEP SMILING
Never train your dog, puppy or adult, when you are angry or in a sour mood. Dogs are very sensitive to human feelings, especially anger, and if your dog senses that you are angry or upset, he will connect your anger with his training and learn to resent or fear his training sessions.

A good example of a dog learning the hard way is the dog who chases the house cat. He is told many times to leave the cat alone, yet he persists in teasing the cat. Then, one day he begins chasing the cat but the cat turns and swipes a claw across the dog's face, leaving him with a painful gash on his nose. The final result is that the dog stops chasing the cat.

PLAN TO PLAY

The puppy should also have regular play and exercise sessions when he is with you or a family member. Exercise for a very young puppy can consist of a short walk around the house or yard. Playing can include fetching games with a large ball or a special toy. (All puppies teethe and need soft things upon which to chew.) Remember to restrict play periods to indoors within his living area (the family room, for example) until he is completely house-trained.

TRAINING EQUIPMENT

COLLAR AND LEAD

Discourage your puppy from chewing on his lead or it may become a difficult habit to break.

For a Bernese Mountain Dog, the collar and lead that you use for training must be one with which you are easily able to work, not too heavy for the dog and perfectly safe.

TREATS

Have a bag of treats on hand. Something nutritious and easy to swallow works best. Use a soft treat, a chunk of cheese or a piece of cooked chicken rather than a dry biscuit. By the time the dog has finished chewing a dry treat, he will forget why he is being rewarded in the first place! In training, rewarding the dog with a food treat will help him associate praise and the treats with learning new behaviors that obviously please his owner. It's important for you to understand that using food rewards will not teach a dog to beg at the table—the only way to teach a dog to beg at the table is to give him food from the table.

TRAINING BEGINS: ASK THE DOG A QUESTION

In order to teach your Berner anything, you must first get his attention. After all, he cannot learn anything if he is looking away from you with his mind on something else.

To get his attention, ask him "School?" and immediately walk over to him and give him a treat as you tell him "Good dog." Wait a minute or two and repeat the routine, this time with a treat in your hand as you approach within a foot of the dog. Do not go directly to him, but stop about a foot short of him and hold out the treat as you ask "School?" He will see you approaching with a treat in your hand and most likely begin walking toward you. As you meet, give him the treat and praise again.

The third time, ask the question, have a treat in your hand and walk only a short distance toward the dog so that he must walk almost all the way to you. As he reaches you, give him the treat and praise again.

By this time, the dog will probably be getting the idea that if he pays attention to you, especially when you ask that question, it will pay off in treats and enjoyable activities for him. In other words, he learns that "school" means doing great things with you that are fun and result in positive attention for him.

Remember that the dog does not understand your verbal language; he only recognizes sounds. Your question translates to a series of sounds for him, and those sounds become the signal to go to you and pay attention; if he does, he will get to interact with you plus receive treats and praise.

THE BASIC COMMANDS

TEACHING SIT

Now that you have the dog's attention, attach his lead and hold it in your left hand and a food treat in your right. Place your food hand at the dog's nose and let him lick the treat but not take it from

TRAINING RULES

If you want to be successful in training your dog, you have four rules to obey yourself:

1. Develop an understanding of how a dog thinks.
2. Do not blame the dog for lack of communication.
3. Define your dog's personality and act accordingly.
4. Have patience and be consistent.

you. Say "Sit" and slowly raise your food hand from in front of the dog's nose up over his head so that he is looking at the ceiling. As he bends his head upward, he will have to bend his knees to maintain his balance. As he bends his knees, he will assume a sit position. At that point, release the food treat and praise lavishly with

Teaching sit to a stubborn Berner may require a little pressure on the dog's rear quarters.

comments such as "Good dog! Good sit!" Remember to always praise enthusiastically, because dogs relish verbal praise from their owners and feel so proud of themselves whenever they accomplish a behavior.

You will not use food forever in getting the dog to obey your commands. Food is only used to teach new behaviors, and once the dog knows what you want when you give a specific command, you will wean him off the food treats but still maintain the verbal praise. The Berner has a strong instinct to please his master and will want to obey for the sake of making his master happy.

TEACHING DOWN
Teaching the down exercise is easy when you understand how

the dog perceives the down position, and it is very difficult when you do not. Dogs perceive the down position as a submissive one, therefore teaching the down exercise using a forceful method can sometimes make the dog develop such a fear of the down that he either runs away when you say "Down" or he attempts to snap at the person who tries to force him down.

Have the dog sit close alongside your left leg, facing in the same direction as you are. Hold the lead in your left hand and a food treat in your right. Now place your left hand lightly on the top of the dog's shoulders where they meet above the spinal cord. Do not push down on the dog's shoulders; simply rest your left hand there so you can guide the dog to lie down close to your left leg rather than to swing away from your side when he drops.

Now place the food hand at the dog's nose, say "Down" very

COMMAND STANCE
Stand up straight and authoritatively when giving your dog commands. Do not issue commands when lying on the floor or lying on your back on the sofa. If you are on your hands and knees when you give a command, your dog will think you are positioning yourself to play.

softly (almost a whisper), and slowly lower the food hand to the dog's front feet. When the food hand reaches the floor, begin moving it forward along the floor in front of the dog. Keep talking softly to the dog, saying things like, "Do you want this treat? You can do this, good dog." Your reassuring tone of voice will help calm the dog as he tries to follow the food hand in order to get the treat.

When the dog's elbows touch the floor, release the food and praise softly. Try to get the dog to maintain that down position for several seconds before you let him sit up again. The goal here is to get the dog to settle down and not feel threatened in the down position.

TEACHING STAY

It is easy to teach the dog to stay in either a sit or a down position. Again, we use food and praise during the teaching process as we help the dog to understand exactly what it is that we are expecting him to do.

To teach the sit/stay, start with the dog sitting on your left side as before and hold the lead in your left hand. Have a food treat in your right hand and place your food hand at the dog's nose. Say "Stay" and step out on your right foot to stand directly in front of the dog, toe to toe, as he licks and nibbles the treat. Be sure to keep

his head facing upward to maintain the sit position. Count to five and then swing around to stand next to the dog again with him on your left. As soon as you get back to the original position, release the food and praise lavishly.

To teach the down/stay, do the down as previously described. As soon as the dog lies down, say "Stay" and step out on your right foot just as you did in the sit/stay. Count to five and then return to stand beside the dog with him on your left side. Release the treat and praise as always.

> **DOUBLE JEOPARDY**
> A dog in jeopardy never lies down. He stays alert on his feet because instinct tells him that he may have to run away or fight for his survival. Therefore, if a dog feels threatened or anxious, he will not lie down. Consequently, it is important to keep the dog calm and relaxed as he learns the down exercise.

CONSISTENCY PAYS OFF

Dogs need consistency in their feeding schedule, exercise and relief visits, and in the verbal commands you use. If you use "Stay" on Monday and "Stay here, please" on Tuesday, you will confuse your dog. Don't demand perfect behavior during training sessions and then let him have the run of the house the rest of the day. Above all, lavish praise on your pet consistently every time he does something right. The more he feels he is pleasing you, the more willing he will be to learn.

stay signal, much the same as the hand signal a cop uses to stop traffic at an intersection. Hold the food treat in your right hand as before, but this time the food is not touching the dog's nose. He will watch the food hand and quickly learn that he is going to get that treat as soon as you return to his side.

When you can stand 3 feet away from your dog for 30 seconds, you can then begin building time and distance in both stays. Eventually, the dog can be expected to remain in the stay position for prolonged periods of time until you return to him or call him to you. Always praise lavishly when he stays.

TEACHING COME

If you make teaching "come" a nice fun experience, you should never have a student that does not love the game or that fails to come when called. The secret, it seems, is never to teach the word "come."

At times when an owner most wants his dog to come when called, the owner is likely to be upset or anxious and he allows these feelings to come through in the tone of his voice when he calls his dog. Hearing that desperation in his owner's voice, the dog fears the results of going to him and therefore either disobeys outright or runs in the opposite direction. The secret,

Within a week or ten days, you can begin to add a bit of distance between you and your dog when you leave him. When you do, use your left hand open with the palm facing the dog as a

therefore, is to teach the dog a game and, when you want him to come to you, simply play the game. It is practically a no-fail solution!

To begin, have several members of your family take a few food treats and each go into a different room in the house. Take turns calling the dog, and each person should celebrate the dog's finding him with a treat and lots of happy praise. When a person calls the dog, he is actually inviting the dog to find him and get a treat as a reward for "winning."

A few turns of the "Where are you?" game and the dog will understand that everyone is playing the game and that each person has a big celebration awaiting his success at locating them. Once he learns to love the game, simply calling out "Where are you?" will bring him running from wherever he is when he hears that all-important question.

The come command is recognized as one of the most important things to teach a dog, but there are trainers who work with thousands of dogs and never teach the actual word "come." Yet these dogs will race to respond to a person who uses the dog's name followed by "Where are you?" For example, a woman has a 9-year-old companion dog who went blind, but who never fails to locate her owner when asked, "Where are you?"

Children, in particular, love to play this game with their dogs. Children can hide in smaller places like a shower stall or bathtub, behind a bed or under a table. The dog needs to work a little bit harder to find these hiding places, but when he does he loves to celebrate with a treat and a tussle with a favorite youngster.

TEACHING HEEL

Heeling means that the dog walks beside the owner without pulling. It takes time and patience on the owner's part to succeed at teaching the dog that he (the owner) will not proceed unless the dog is walking calmly beside him. Pulling out ahead on the lead is definitely not acceptable.

Begin by holding the lead in your left hand as the dog sits beside your left leg. Move the loop end of the lead to your right hand but keep your left hand short on the lead so it keeps the dog in close next to you.

"COME" . . . BACK
Never call your dog to come to you for a correction or scold him when he reaches you. That is the quickest way to turn a come command into "Go away fast!" Dogs think only in the present tense, and your dog will connect the scolding with coming to you, not with the misbehavior of a few moments earlier.

> ## PRACTICE MAKES PERFECT!
> - Have training lessons with your dog every day in several short segments—three to five times a day for a few minutes at a time is ideal.
> - Do not have long practice sessions. The dog will become easily bored.
> - Never practice when you are tired, ill, worried or in an otherwise negative mood. This will transmit to the dog and may have an adverse effect on his performance.
>
>   Think fun, short and above all *positive!* End each session on a high note, rather than a failed exercise, and make sure to give a lot of praise. Enjoy the training and help your dog enjoy it, too.

The goal of heel training is to have your Berner walk beside you on lead without pulling. The rewards of a properly heel-trained dog are evident every time you take your dog for a peaceful, leisurely stroll.

Say "Heel" and step forward on your left foot. Keep the dog close to you and take three steps. Stop and have the dog sit next to you in what we now call the heel position. Praise verbally, but do not touch the dog. Hesitate a moment and begin again with "Heel," taking three steps and stopping, at which point the dog is told to sit again.

Your goal here is to have the dog walk those three steps without pulling on the lead. Once he will walk calmly beside you for three steps without pulling, increase the number of steps you take to five. When he will walk politely beside you while you take five steps, you can increase the length of your walk to ten

steps. Keep increasing the length of your stroll until the dog will walk quietly beside you without pulling as long as you want him to heel. When you stop heeling, indicate to the dog that the exercise is over by verbally praising as you pet him and say "OK, good dog." The "OK" is used as a release word, meaning that the exercise is finished and the dog is free to relax.

If you are dealing with a pup who insists on pulling you around, simply "put on your brakes" and stand your ground until the pup realizes that the two of you are not going anywhere until he is beside you and moving at your pace, not his. It may take some time just standing there to convince the dog that you are the leader and you will be the one to decide on the direction and speed of your travel.

Given the strength and mass of an adult Berner, owners are well advised to heel train before the dog weighs 100 pounds.

Each time the dog looks up at you or slows down to give a slack lead between the two of you, quietly praise him and say, "Good heel. Good dog." Eventually, the dog will begin to respond and within a few days he will be walking politely beside you without pulling on the lead. At first, the training sessions should be kept short and very positive; soon the dog will be able to walk nicely with you for increasingly longer distances. Remember also to give the dog free time and the opportunity to run and play when you have finished heel practice.

WEANING OFF FOOD IN TRAINING

Food is used in training new behaviors. Once the dog understands what behavior goes with a specific command, it is time to start weaning him off the food

Heeling politely at your side, your Berner will be a gentleman every time you take a walk.

treats. At first, give a treat after each exercise. Then, start to give a treat only after every other exercise. Mix up the times when you offer a food reward and the times when you only offer praise so that the dog will never know when he is going to receive both food and praise and when he is going to receive only praise. This is called a variable-ratio-reward system and it proves successful because there is always the chance that the owner will produce a treat, so the dog never stops trying for that reward. No matter what, *always* give verbal praise.

OBEDIENCE CLASSES

It is a good idea to enroll in an obedience class if one is available in your area. If yours is a show dog, conformation showing classes would be more appropriate. Many areas have dog clubs

---

TUG OF WALK?

If you begin teaching the heel by taking long walks and letting the dog pull you along, he misinterprets this action as an acceptable form of taking a walk. When you pull back on the leash to counteract his pulling, he reads that tug as a signal to pull even harder!

FAMILY TIES

If you have other pets in the home and/or interact often with the pets of friends and other family members, your pup will respond to those pets in much the same manner as you do. It is only when you show fear of or resentment toward another animal that he will act fearful or unfriendly.

that offer basic obedience training as well as preparatory classes for obedience competition. There are also local dog trainers who offer similar classes.

OTHER ACTIVITIES FOR LIFE

Whether a dog is trained in the structured environment of a class or alone with his owner at home, there are many activities that can bring fun and rewards to both owner and dog once they have mastered basic control.

Teaching the dog to help out around the home, in the yard or on the farm provides great satisfaction to both dog and owner. In addition, the dog's help makes life a little easier for his owner and raises his stature as a valued companion to his family. It helps give the dog a purpose by occupying his mind and providing an outlet for his energy.

Backpacking is another exciting and healthy activity that the dog can be taught without assistance from more than his owner. The exercise of walking and climbing is good for man and dog alike, and the bond that they develop together is priceless. The Berner can compete for a Working Pack Dog title at the Greater Swiss Mountain Dog Club of America. To earn the award, the dog must carry 20 or 30% of his body weight.

At obedience trials, dogs can earn titles at various levels of competition. The beginning levels of competition include basic behaviors such as sit, down, heel, etc. The more advanced levels of competition include jumping, retrieving, scent discrimination and signal work. The advanced levels require a dog and owner to put a lot of time and effort into their training and the titles that can be earned at these levels of competition are very prestigious.

If you are interested in participating in organized competition with your Bernese, there are activities other than obedience in which you and your dog can become involved. Agility is a popular sport where dogs run through an obstacle course that includes various jumps, tunnels and other exercises to test the dog's speed and coordination. The owners run beside their dogs to give commands and to guide them through the course. Although competitive, the focus is on fun—it's fun to do, fun to watch and great exercise.

If a Bernese owner wants to take advantage of the breed's drafting ability, carting is the most popular mountain-dog activity. There are clubs that organize carting events, all of which are terrific enjoyment for dog and owner, some of which are competitive with prizes.

Like carting, weight pulls are an exciting, social event for your dog that does not require as much training as an agility trial. In order for a dog to participate in a weight pull, you will need a freight harness, a strong collar (never prong) and a leash. To practice you will need a pulling line, plastic sledge and some make-shift weights. To train your dog to pull, he must obey a stay command, which is required so that the dog (attached to the cart) doesn't start pulling until you walk to the finish line. Accustom the dog to the harness and to the sensation of pulling a cart or some other weight (a car tire is a good starting point). The dog needs to obey the following commands by voice and hand signal: Stand-stay, heel,

come, down and down-stay. The course on most weight pulls is 16 feet in length, so you must practice with your dog to pull at least this distance. Contact the International Weight Pull Association at www.iwpa.net for more information about pulls in your area.

FEAR AGGRESSION

Pups who are subjected to physical abuse during training commonly end up with behavioral problems as adults. One common result of abuse is fear aggression, in which a dog will lash out, bare his teeth, snarl and finally bite someone by whom he feels threatened. For example, your daughter may be playing with the dog one afternoon. As they play hide-and-seek, she backs the dog into a corner and, as she attempts to tease him playfully, he bites her hand. Examine the cause of this behavior. Did your daughter ever hit the dog? Did someone who resembles your daughter hit or scream at the dog?

Fortunately, fear aggression is relatively easy to correct. Have your daughter engage in only positive activities with the dog, such as feeding, petting and walking. She should not give any corrections or negative feedback. If the dog still growls or cowers away from her, allow someone else to accompany them. After approximately one week, the dog should feel that he can rely on her for many positive things, and he will also be prevented from reacting fearfully towards anyone who might resemble her.

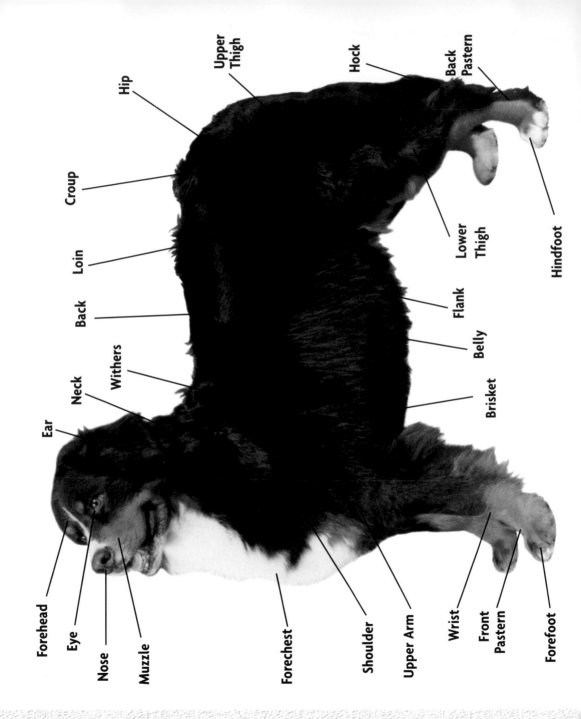

Upper Thigh

Hip

Hock

Back Pastern

Croup

Lower Thigh

Hindfoot

Loin

Back

Flank

Belly

Withers

Neck

Brisket

Ear

Forehead

Eye

Nose

Muzzle

Forechest

Shoulder

Upper Arm

Wrist

Front Pastern

Forefoot

PHYSICAL STRUCTURE OF THE BERNESE MOUNTAIN DOG

Dogs suffer from many of the same physical illnesses as people. They might even share many of the same psychological problems. Since people usually know more about human diseases than canine maladies, many of the terms used in this chapter will be familiar but not necessarily those used by veterinarians. We will use the term *x-ray*, instead of the more acceptable term *radiograph*. We will also use the familiar term *symptoms* even though dogs don't have symptoms, which are verbal descriptions of the patient's feelings; dogs have *clinical signs*. Since dogs can't speak, we have to look for clinical signs...but we still use the term *symptoms* in this book.

As a general rule, medicine is *practiced*. That term is not arbitrary. Medicine is a constantly changing art as we learn more and more about genetics, electronic aids (like CAT scans and MRIs) and daily laboratory advances. There are many dog maladies, like canine hip dysplasia, which are not universally treated in the same manner. Some veterinarians opt for surgery more often than others do.

SELECTING A VETERINARIAN

Your selection of a veterinarian should be based not only upon personality and skill with large-breed dogs, especially Berners, but upon his convenience to your home. You want a vet who is close because you might have emergencies or need to make multiple visits for treatments. You want a vet who has services that you might require such as tattooing and grooming, as well as sophisticated pet supplies and a good reputation for ability

---

VITAL SIGNS

A dog's normal temperature is 101.5 degrees Fahrenheit. A range of between 100.0 and 102.5 degrees should be considered normal, as each dog's body sets its own temperature. It will be helpful if you take your dog's temperature when you know he is healthy and record it. Then, when you suspect that he is not feeling well, you will have a normal figure to compare the abnormal temperature against.

The normal pulse rate for a dog is between 100 and 125 beats per minute.

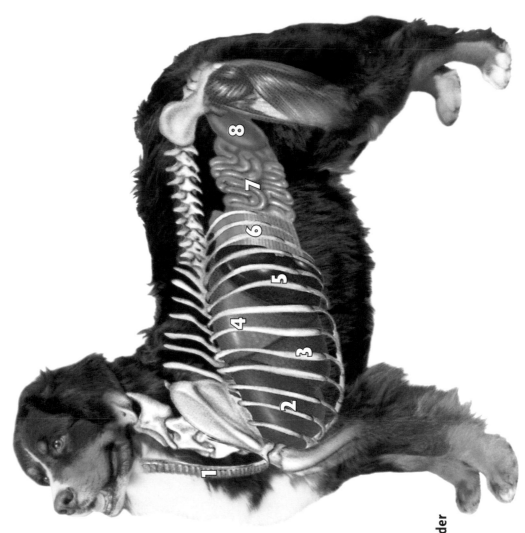

1. Esophagus
2. Lungs
3. Gall Bladder
4. Liver
5. Kidney
6. Stomach
7. Intestines
8. Urinary Bladder

INTERNAL ORGANS OF THE BERNESE MOUNTAIN DOG

and responsiveness. There is nothing more frustrating than having to wait a day or more to get a response from your veterinarian.

All veterinarians are licensed and their diplomas and/or certificates should be displayed in their waiting rooms. There are, however, many veterinary specialties that usually require further studies and internships. There are specialists in heart problems (veterinary cardiologists), skin problems (veterinary

Breakdown of Veterinary Income by Category

2%	Dentistry
4%	Radiology
12%	Surgery
15%	Vaccinations
19%	Laboratory
23%	Examinations
25%	Medicines

A typical vet's income, categorized according to services performed. This survey dealt with small-animal (pets) practices.

DISEASE REFERENCE CHART

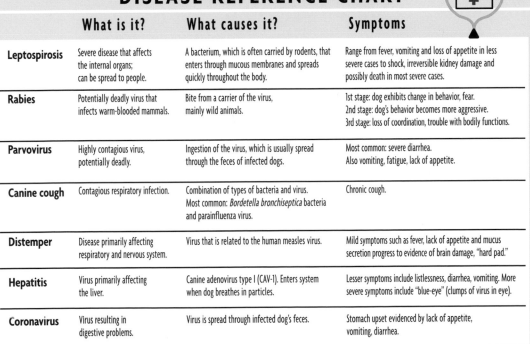

	What is it?	What causes it?	Symptoms
Leptospirosis	Severe disease that affects the internal organs; can be spread to people.	A bacterium, which is often carried by rodents, that enters through mucous membranes and spreads quickly throughout the body.	Range from fever, vomiting and loss of appetite in less severe cases to shock, irreversible kidney damage and possibly death in most severe cases.
Rabies	Potentially deadly virus that infects warm-blooded mammals.	Bite from a carrier of the virus, mainly wild animals.	1st stage: dog exhibits change in behavior, fear. 2nd stage: dog's behavior becomes more aggressive. 3rd stage: loss of coordination, trouble with bodily functions.
Parvovirus	Highly contagious virus, potentially deadly.	Ingestion of the virus, which is usually spread through the feces of infected dogs.	Most common: severe diarrhea. Also vomiting, fatigue, lack of appetite.
Canine cough	Contagious respiratory infection.	Combination of types of bacteria and virus. Most common: *Bordetella bronchiseptica* bacteria and parainfluenza virus.	Chronic cough.
Distemper	Disease primarily affecting respiratory and nervous system.	Virus that is related to the human measles virus.	Mild symptoms such as fever, lack of appetite and mucus secretion progress to evidence of brain damage, "hard pad."
Hepatitis	Virus primarily affecting the liver.	Canine adenovirus type I (CAV-1). Enters system when dog breathes in particles.	Lesser symptoms include listlessness, diarrhea, vomiting. More severe symptoms include "blue-eye" (clumps of virus in eye).
Coronavirus	Virus resulting in digestive problems.	Virus is spread through infected dog's feces.	Stomach upset evidenced by lack of appetite, vomiting, diarrhea.

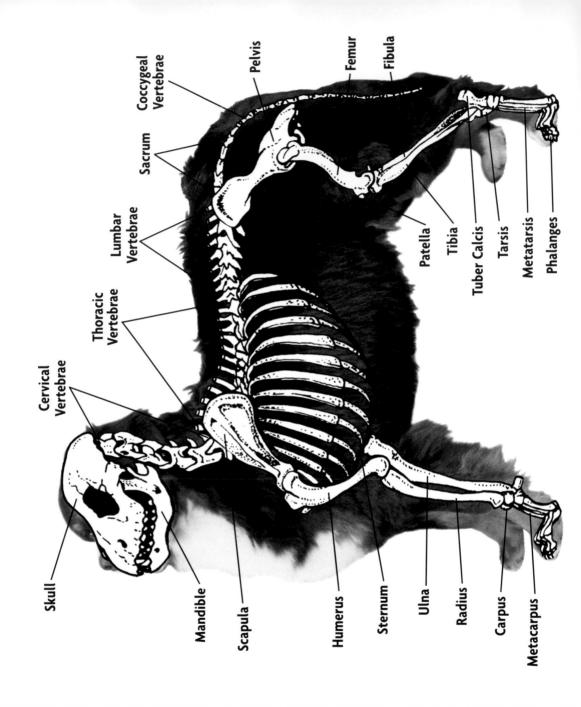

SKELETAL STRUCTURE OF THE BERNESE MOUNTAIN DOG

dermatologists), teeth and gum problems (veterinary dentists), eye problems (veterinary ophthalmologists) and x-rays (veterinary radiologists), as well as vets who have specialties in bones, muscles or certain organs. Most veterinarians do routine surgery such as neutering, stitching up wounds and docking tails for those breeds in which such is required for show purposes.

When the problem affecting your dog is serious, it is not unusual or impudent to get another medical opinion, although it's a good idea to advise the vets concerned about this. You might also want to compare costs among several veterinarians. Sophisticated health care and veterinary

PET ADVANTAGES

If you do not intend to show or breed your new puppy, your veterinarian will probably recommend that you spay your female or neuter your male. Some people believe neutering leads to weight gain, but if you feed and exercise your dog properly, this is easily avoided. Spaying or neutering can actually have many positive outcomes, such as:

- training becomes easier, as the dog focuses less on the urge to mate and more on you!
- females are protected from unplanned pregnancy as well as ovarian and uterine cancers.
- males are guarded from testicular tumors and have a reduced risk of developing prostate cancer.

Talk to your vet regarding the right age to spay/neuter and other aspects of the procedure.

services can be very costly. It is not infrequent that important decisions are based upon financial considerations.

PREVENTATIVE MEDICINE

It is much easier, less costly and more effective to practice preventative medicine than to fight bouts of illness and disease. Properly bred puppies come from parents who were selected based upon their genetic-disease profiles. Their dam should have

Zoonoses are diseases passed from animal to human. If you take proper care of your dog, you should not have to worry about ever acquiring an illness from your dog.

Normal hairs of a dog enlarged 200 times original size. The cuticle (outer covering) is clean and healthy. Unlike human hair that grows from the base, a dog's hair also grows from the end, as shown in the inset.

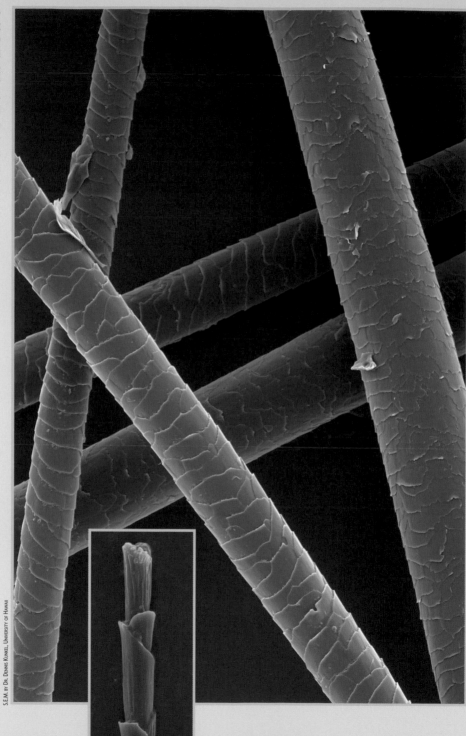

been vaccinated, free of all internal and external parasites and properly nourished. The dam can pass on disease resistance to her puppies, which can last for eight to ten weeks. She can also pass on parasites and many infections. It's advisable to know everything about the dam's health.

VACCINATION SCHEDULING

Most vaccinations are given by injection and should only be done by a veterinarian. Both he and you should keep a record of the date of the injection, the identification of the vaccine and the amount given. Some vets give a first vaccination at eight weeks, but most dog breeders prefer the course not to commence until about ten

HEALTH AND VACCINATION SCHEDULE

AGE IN WEEKS:	6TH	8TH	10TH	12TH	14TH	16TH	20-24TH	52ND
Worm Control	✔	✔	✔	✔	✔	✔	✔	
Neutering							✔	
Heartworm		✔		✔		✔	✔	
Parvovirus	✔		✔		✔		✔	✔
Distemper		✔		✔		✔		✔
Hepatitis		✔		✔		✔		✔
Leptospirosis								✔
Parainfluenza	✔		✔		✔			✔
Dental Examination		✔					✔	✔
Complete Physical		✔					✔	✔
Coronavirus				✔			✔	✔
Canine Cough	✔							
Hip Dysplasia								✔
Rabies							✔	

Vaccinations are not instantly effective. It takes about two weeks for the dog's immune system to develop antibodies. Most vaccinations require annual booster shots. Your vet should guide you in this regard.

weeks because of negating any antibodies passed on by the dam. The vaccination scheduling is usually based on a 15-day cycle. You must take your vet's advice regarding when to vaccinate as this may differ according to the vaccine used. Most vaccinations immunize your puppy against viruses.

The usual vaccines contain immunizing doses of several different viruses such as distemper, parvovirus, parainfluenza and hepatitis although some veterinarians recommend separate vaccines for each disease. There are other vaccines available when the puppy is at risk. You should rely upon professional advice. This is especially true for the booster-shot program. Most vaccination programs require a booster when the puppy is a year old and once a year thereafter. In some cases, circumstances may require more or less frequent immunizations. Canine cough, more formally known as tracheobronchitis, is treated with a vaccine that is sprayed into the dog's nostrils. Canine cough is usually included in routine vaccination, but this is often not so effective as for other major diseases.

WEANING TO FIVE MONTHS OLD
Puppies should be weaned by the time they are about two months old. A puppy that remains for at

---

KNOW WHEN TO POSTPONE A VACCINATION
While the visit to the vet is costly, it is never advisable to update a vaccination when visiting with a sick or pregnant dog. Vaccinations should be avoided for all elderly dogs. If your dog is showing the signs of any illness or any medical condition, no matter how serious or mild, including skin irritations, do not vaccinate. Likewise, a lame dog should never be vaccinated; any dog undergoing surgery or on any immunosuppressant drugs should not be vaccinated until fully recovered.

---

least eight weeks with his dam and littermates usually adapts better to other dogs and people later in his life.

Some new owners have their puppy examined by a veterinarian immediately, which is a good idea. Vaccination programs usually begin when the puppy is very young.

The puppy will have his teeth examined and have his skeletal conformation and general health checked prior to certification by the veterinarian. Puppies in certain breeds have problems with their kneecaps, cataracts and other eye problems, heart murmurs and undescended testicles. They may also have personality problems and your veterinarian might have training in temperament evaluation.

FIVE TO TWELVE MONTHS OF AGE

Unless you intend to breed or show your dog, neutering the puppy at six months of age is recommended. Discuss this with your vet. Neutering/spaying has proven to be extremely beneficial to both male and female puppies, respectively. Besides eliminating the possibility of pregnancy, pyometra and testicular cancer, it inhibits (but does not prevent) breast cancer in bitches and prostate cancer in male dogs. Under no circumstances should a bitch be spayed prior to her first season.

Your veterinarian should provide your puppy with a thorough dental evaluation at six months of age, ascertaining whether all of the permanent teeth have erupted properly. A home dental-care regimen should be initiated at six months, including brushing weekly and providing good dental devices (such as nylon bones). Regular dental care promotes healthy teeth, fresh breath and a longer life.

OVER ONE YEAR OF AGE

Once a year, your dog should visit the vet for an examination and vaccination boosters, if needed. Some vets recommend blood tests, thyroid level check and dental evaluation to accompany these annual visits. A thorough clinical evaluation by the vet can provide critical background information for your dog. Blood tests are often performed at one year of age, and dental examinations around the third or fourth birthday. In the long run, quality preventative care for your pet can save money, teeth and lives.

SKIN PROBLEMS IN BERNESE MOUNTAIN DOGS

Veterinarians are consulted by dog owners for skin problems

HOW TO PREVENT BLOAT

Research has confirmed that the structure of deep-chested breeds contributes to their predisposition to bloat. Nevertheless, there are several precautions that you can take to reduce the risk of this condition:

- Feed your dog twice daily rather than offer one big meal.
- Do not exercise your dog for at least one hour before and two hours after he has eaten.
- Make certain that your dog is calm and not overly excited while he is eating. It has been proven that nervous or overly excited dogs are more prone to develop bloat.
- Add a small portion of moist meat product to his dry food ration.
- Serve his meals in an elevated bowl stand, which avoids the dog's craning his neck while eating.
- To prevent your dog from gobbling his food too quickly, and thereby swallowing air, put some large (unswallowable) toys into his bowl so that he will have to eat around them to get his food.

more than any other group of diseases or maladies. Dogs' skin is almost as sensitive as human skin and both suffer almost the same ailments (though the occurrence of acne in dogs is rare!). For this reason, veterinary dermatology has developed into a specialty practiced by many veterinarians.

Since many skin problems have visual symptoms that are almost identical, it requires the skill of an experienced veterinary dermatologist to identify and cure many of the more severe skin disorders. Pet shops sell many treatments for skin problems, but most of the treatments are directed at symptoms and not

A SKUNKY PROBLEM

Have you noticed your dog dragging his rump along the floor? If so, it is likely that his anal sacs are impacted or possibly infected. The anal sacs are small pouches located on both sides of the anus under the skin and muscles. They are about the size and shape of a grape and contain a foul-smelling liquid. Their contents are usually emptied when the dog has a bowel movement but, if not emptied completely, they will impact, which will cause your dog much pain. Fortunately, your veterinarian can tend to this problem easily by draining the sacs for the dog. Be aware that your dog might also empty his anal sacs in cases of extreme fright.

Don't Eat the Daisies!

Many plants and flowers are beautiful to look at, but can be highly toxic if ingested by your dog. Reactions range from abdominal pain and vomiting to convulsions and death. If the following plants are in your home, remove them. If they are outside your house or in your garden, avoid accidents by making sure your dog is never left unsupervised in those locations.

Azalea	Dumb cane	Mescal bean
Belladonna	Dutchman's breeches	Mushrooms
Bird of paradise	Elephant's ear	Nightshade
Bulbs	Hydrangea	Philodendron
Calla lily	Jack-in-the-pulpit	Poinsettia
Cardinal flower	Jasmine	*Prunus* species
Castor bean	Jimsonweed	Tobacco
Chinaberry tree	Larkspur	Yellow jasmine
Daphne	Laurel	Yews, *Taxus* species
	Lily of the valley	

Number-One Killer Disease in Dogs: CANCER

In every age, there is a word associated with a disease or plague that causes humans to shudder. In the 21st century, that word is "cancer." Just as cancer is the leading cause of death in humans, it claims nearly half the lives of dogs that die from a natural disease as well as half the dogs that die over the age of ten years.

Described as a genetic disease, cancer becomes a greater risk as the dog ages. Vets and dog owners have become increasingly aware of the threat of cancer to dogs. Statistics reveal that one dog in every five will develop cancer, the most common of which is skin cancer. Many cancers, including prostate, ovarian and breast cancer, can be avoided by spaying and neutering our dogs by the age of six months.

Early detection of cancer can save or extend a dog's life, so it is absolutely vital for owners to have their dogs examined by a qualified vet or oncologist immediately upon detection of any abnormality. Certain dietary guidelines have also proven to reduce the onset and spread of cancer. Foods based on fish rather than beef, due to the presence of Omega-3 fatty acids, are recommended. Other amino acids such as glutamine have significant benefits for canines, particularly those breeds that show a greater susceptibility to cancer.

Cancer management and treatments promise hope for future generations of canines. Since the disease is genetic, breeders should never breed a dog whose parents, grandparents and any related siblings have developed cancer. It is difficult to know whether to exclude an otherwise healthy dog from a breeding program, as the disease does not manifest itself until the dog's senior years.

RECOGNIZE CANCER WARNING SIGNS

Since early detection can possibly rescue your dog from becoming a cancer statistic, it is essential for owners to recognize the possible signs and seek the assistance of a qualified professional.

- Abnormal bumps or lumps that continue to grow
- Bleeding or discharge from any body cavity
- Persistent stiffness or lameness
- Recurrent sores or sores that do not heal
- Inappetence
- Breathing difficulties
- Weight loss
- Bad breath or odors
- General malaise and fatigue
- Eating and swallowing problems
- Difficulty urinating and defecating

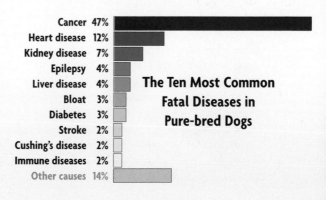

Disease	%
Cancer	47%
Heart disease	12%
Kidney disease	7%
Epilepsy	4%
Liver disease	4%
Bloat	3%
Diabetes	3%
Stroke	2%
Cushing's disease	2%
Immune diseases	2%
Other causes	14%

The Ten Most Common Fatal Diseases in Pure-bred Dogs

the underlying problem(s). If your dog is suffering from a skin disorder, you should seek professional assistance as quickly as possible. As with all diseases, the earlier a problem is identified and treated, the more successful is the cure.

HEREDITARY SKIN DISORDERS
Veterinary dermatologists are currently researching a number of skin disorders that are believed to have hereditary bases. These inherited diseases are transmitted by both parents, who appear (phenotypically) normal but have a recessive gene for the disease, meaning that they carry, but are not affected by, the disease. These diseases pose serious problems to breeders because in some instances there is no method of identifying carriers. Often the secondary diseases associated with

The Eyes Have It!

Eye disease is more prevalent among dogs than most people think, ranging from slight infections that are easily treated to serious complications that can lead to permanent sight loss. Eye diseases need veterinary attention in their early stages to prevent irreparable damage. This list provides descriptions of some common eye diseases:

Cataracts: Symptoms are white or gray discoloration of the eye lens and pupil, which causes fuzzy or completely obscured vision. Surgical treatment is required to remove the damaged lens and replace it with an artificial one.

Conjunctivitis: An inflammation of the mucus membrane that lines the eye socket, leaving the eyes red and puffy with excessive discharge. This condition is easily treated with antibiotics.

Corneal damage: The cornea is the transparent covering of the iris and pupil. Injuries are difficult to detect, but manifest themselves in surface abnormality, redness, pain and discharge. Most infections of the cornea are treated with antibiotics and require immediate medical attention.

Dry eye: This condition is caused by deficient production of tears that lubricate and protect the eye surface. A telltale sign is yellow-green discharge. Left undiagnosed, your dog will experience considerable pain, infections and possibly blindness. Dry eye is commonly treated with antibiotics, although more advanced cases may require surgery.

Glaucoma: This is caused by excessive fluid pressure in the eye. Symptoms are red eyes, gray or blue discoloration, pain, enlarged eyeballs and loss of vision. Antibiotics sometimes help, but surgery may be needed.

these skin conditions are even more debilitating than the disorder itself, including cancers and respiratory problems.

Among the hereditary skin disorders, for which the mode of inheritance is known, are acrodermatitis, cutaneous asthenia (Ehlers-Danlos syndrome), sebaceous adenitis, cyclic hematopoiesis, dermatomyositis, IgA deficiency, color dilution alopecia and nodular dermatofibrosis. Some of these disorders are limited to one or two breeds and others affect a large number of breeds. All inherited diseases must be diagnosed and treated by a veterinary specialist.

Parasite Bites

Many of us are allergic to insect bites. The bites itch, erupt and may even become infected. Dogs have the same reaction to fleas, ticks and/or mites. When an insect lands on you, you have the chance to whisk it away with your hand. Unfortunately, when your dog is bitten by a flea, tick or mite, he can only scratch it away or bite it. By the time the dog has been bitten, the parasite has done some of its damage. It may also have laid eggs to cause further problems in the near future. The itching from parasite bites is probably due to the saliva injected into the site when the parasite sucks the dog's blood.

DENTAL HEALTH

A dental examination is in order when the dog is between six months and one year of age so that any permanent teeth that have erupted incorrectly can be corrected. It is important to begin a brushing routine at home, using dental-care products made for dogs, such as special toothbrushes and toothpaste. Durable nylon and safe edible chews should be a part of your puppy's arsenal for good health, good teeth and pleasant breath. The vast majority of dogs three to four years old and older has diseases of the gums from lack of dental attention. Using the various types of dental chews can be very effective in controlling dental plaque.

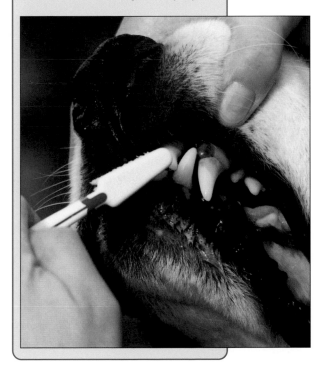

AUTO-IMMUNE SKIN CONDITIONS
Auto-immune skin conditions
are commonly referred to as
being allergic to yourself, while
allergies are usually inflamma-
tory reactions to an outside stim-
ulus. For unknown reasons,
Berners are more susceptible to
auto-immune diseases than are
other breeds. Auto-immune
diseases cause serious damage to
the tissues that are involved.
Berners have been cited with
immune-mediated polyarthritis
(IMPA), which could be related
to systematic lupus erythemato-
sus, and present itself as
inflamed joints.

The best known auto-
immune disease is lupus, which

Sometimes an itch is just an itch. Be careful that your Berner's plush puppy coat doesn't become a nesting place for fleas and other parasites.

> ## PARVO FOR THE COURSE
> Canine parvovirus is an highly conta-
> gious disease that attacks puppies
> and older dogs. Spread through
> contact with infected feces,
> parvovirus causes bloody diarrhea,
> vomiting, heart damage, dehydration,
> shock and death. To prevent this
> tragedy, breeders have their puppies
> begin their series of vaccinations at
> six to eight weeks of age. Be aware
> that the virus is easily spread and is
> carried on a dog's hair, feet, water
> bowls and other objects, as well as
> on people's shoes and clothing.

affects people as well as dogs.
The symptoms are variable and
may affect the kidneys, bones,
blood chemistry and skin. It can
be fatal to both dogs and
humans, though it is not thought
to be transmissible. It is usually
successfully treated with cortisone, prednisone or a similar
corticosteroid, but extensive use
of these drugs can have harmful
side effects.

ACRAL LICK GRANULOMA
Many large dogs have a very
poorly understood syndrome
called acral lick granuloma. The
manifestation of the problem is
the dog's tireless attack at a
specific area of the body, almost
always the legs or paws. They
lick so intensively that they

remove the hair and skin, leaving an ugly, large wound. Tiny protuberances, which are outgrowths of new capillaries, bead on the surface of the wound. Owners who notice their dogs' biting and chewing at their extremities should have the vet determine the cause. If acral lick granuloma is identified, although there is no absolute cure, corticosteroids are one common treatment.

AIRBORNE ALLERGIES

Just as humans have hay fever, rose fever and other fevers from which they suffer during the pollinating season, many dogs suffer from the same allergies. When the pollen count is high, your dog might suffer but don't expect him to sneeze and have a runny nose as a human would. Dogs react to pollen allergies the same way they react to fleas—they scratch and bite themselves.

Dogs, like humans, can be tested for allergens. Discuss the testing with your veterinary dermatologist.

FOOD PROBLEMS

FOOD ALLERGIES

Dogs can be allergic to many foods that are best-sellers and highly recommended by breeders and veterinarians. Changing the brand of food that you buy may not eliminate the problem if the

THE GRASS WITHERS ...
Dogs who have been exposed to lawns sprayed with herbicides have double and triple the rate of malignant lymphoma. Town dogs are especially at risk, as they are exposed to tailored lawns and gardens. Dogs perspire and absorb through their footpads. Be careful where your dog walks and always avoid any area that appears yellowed from chemical overspray.

element to which the dog is allergic is contained in the new brand.

Recognizing a food allergy is difficult. Humans vomit or have rashes when they eat a food to which they are allergic. Dogs neither vomit nor (usually)

Dogs pant to cool off, unlike humans who sweat. Never leave your dog outside in hot weather without shelter and plenty of clean water.

develop a rash. They react in the same manner as they do to an airborne or flea allergy; they itch, scratch and bite, thus making the diagnosis extremely difficult. While pollen allergies and parasite bites are usually seasonal, food allergies are year-round problems.

> **FAT OR FICTION?**
> The myth that dogs need extra fat in their diets can be harmful. Should your vet recommend extra fat, use safflower oil instead of animal oils. Safflower oil has been shown to be less likely to cause allergic reactions.

FOOD INTOLERANCE

Food intolerance is the inability of the dog to completely digest certain foods. Puppies that may have done very well on their mother's milk may not do well on cow's milk. The result of this food intolerance may be loose bowels, passing gas and stomach pains. These are the only obvious symptoms of food intolerance and that makes diagnosis difficult.

TREATING FOOD PROBLEMS

It is possible to handle food allergies and food intolerance yourself. Put your dog on a diet that he has never had. Obviously if he has never eaten this new food he can't have been allergic or intolerant of it. Start with a single ingredient that is not in the dog's diet at the present time. Ingredients like chopped beef or chicken are common in dogs' diets, so try something different like lamb and rice or fish. Keep the dog on this diet (with no additives) for a month. If the symptoms of food allergy or intolerance disappear, chances are your dog has a food allergy.

Don't think that the single ingredient cured the problem. You still must find a suitable diet and ascertain which ingredient in the old diet was objectionable. This is most easily done by adding ingredients to the new diet one at a time. Let the dog stay on the modified diet for a month before you add another ingredient. Eventually, you will determine the ingredient that caused the adverse reaction.

An alternative method is to carefully study the ingredients in the diet to which your dog is allergic or intolerant. Identify the main ingredient in this diet and eliminate the main ingredient by buying a different food that does not have that ingredient. Keep experimenting until the symptoms disappear after one month on the new diet.

Fatty Risks

Large breeds like the Bernese Mountain Dog can frequently suffer from obesity. Studies show that nearly 30% of our dogs are overweight, primarily from high caloric intake and low energy expenditure. The hound and sporting breeds are the most likely affected, and females are at a greater risk of obesity than males. Pet dogs that are neutered are twice as prone to obesity as intact, whole dogs.

Regardless of breed, your dog should have a visible "waist" behind his rib cage and in front of the hindlegs. There should be no fatty deposits on his hips or over his rump, and his abdomen should not be extended.

Veterinary specialists link obesity with respiratory problems, cardiac disease and liver dysfunction as well as low sperm count and abnormal estrous cycles in breeding animals. Other complications include musculoskeletal disease (including arthritis), decreased immune competence, diabetes mellitus, hypothyroidism, pancreatitis and dermatosis. Other studies have indicated that excess fat leads to heat stress, as obese dogs cannot regulate their body temperatures as well as normal-weight dogs.

Don't be discouraged if you discover that your dog has a heart problem or a neurological condition requiring special attention. It is possible to tend to his special medical needs. Veterinary specialists focus on areas such as cardiology, neurology and oncology. Veterinary medical associations require rigorous training and experience before granting certification in a specialty. Consulting a specialist may offer you greater peace of mind when seeking treatment for your dog.

A male dog flea, *Ctenocephalides canis.*

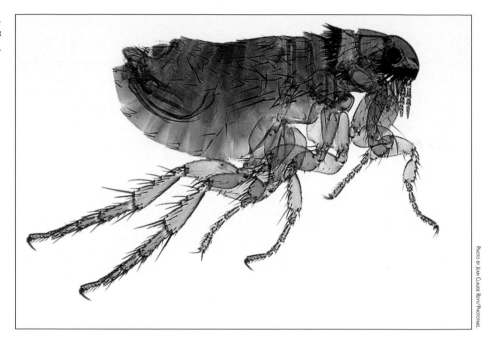

EXTERNAL PARASITES

FLEAS
Of all the problems to which dogs are prone, none is more well known and frustrating than fleas. Flea infestation is relatively simple to cure but difficult to prevent. Parasites that are harbored inside the body are a bit more difficult to eradicate but they are easier to control.

To control flea infestation, you have to understand the flea's life cycle. Fleas are often thought of as a summertime problem, but centrally heated homes have changed the patterns and fleas can be found at any time of the year. The most effective method of flea control is a two-stage approach: one stage to kill the adult fleas, and the other to control the development of pre-adult fleas. Unfortunately, no single active ingredient is effective against all stages of the life cycle.

FLEA KILLER CAUTION—"POISON"
Flea-killers are poisonous. You should not spray these toxic chemicals on areas of a dog's body that he licks, including his genitals and his face. Flea killers taken internally are a better answer, but check with your vet in case internal therapy is not advised for your dog.

LIFE CYCLE STAGES

During its life, a flea will pass through four life stages: egg, larva, pupa or nymph and adult. The adult stage is the most visible and irritating stage of the flea life cycle, and this is why the majority of flea-control products concentrate on this stage. The fact is that adult fleas account for only 1% of the total flea population, and the other 99% exist in pre-adult stages, i.e., eggs, larvae and nymphs. The pre-adult stages are barely visible to the naked eye.

THE LIFE CYCLE OF THE FLEA

Eggs are laid on the dog, usually in quantities of about 20 or 30, several times a day. The adult female flea must have a blood meal before each egg-laying session. When first laid, the eggs will cling to the dog's hair, as the eggs are still moist. However, they will quickly dry out and fall from the dog, especially if the dog moves around or scratches. Many eggs will fall off in the dog's favorite area or an area in which he spends a lot of time, such as his bed.

Once the eggs fall from the dog onto the carpet or furniture, they will hatch into larvae. This takes from one to ten days. Larvae are not particularly mobile and will usually travel only a few inches from where they hatch. However, they do have a tendency to move away from bright light and heavy

**EN GARDE:
CATCHING FLEAS OFF GUARD!**
Consider the following ways to arm yourself against fleas:
- Add a small amount of pennyroyal or eucalyptus oil to your dog's bath. These natural remedies repel fleas.
- Supplement your dog's food with fresh garlic (minced or grated) and a hearty amount of brewer's yeast, both of which ward off fleas.
- Use a flea comb on your dog daily. Submerge fleas in a cup of bleach to kill them quickly.
- Confine the dog to only a few rooms to limit the spread of fleas in the home.
- Vacuum daily...and get all of the crevices! Dispose of the bag every few days until the problem is under control.
- Wash your dog's bedding daily. Cover cushions where your dog sleeps with towels, and wash the towels often.

traffic—under furniture and behind doors are common places to find high quantities of flea larvae.

The flea larvae feed on dead organic matter, including adult flea feces, until they are ready to change into adult fleas. Fleas will usually remain as larvae for around seven days. After this period, the larvae will pupate into protective pupae. While inside the pupae, the larvae will undergo metamorphosis and change into adult fleas. This can take as little time as a few days, but the adult fleas can remain inside the pupae waiting to hatch for up to two years. The pupae are signaled to hatch by certain stimuli, such as physical pressure—the pupae's being stepped on, heat from an animal's lying on the pupae or increased carbon-dioxide levels and vibrations—indicating that a suitable host is available.

Once hatched, the adult flea must feed within a few days. Once the adult flea finds a host, it will not leave voluntarily. It only becomes dislodged by grooming or the host animal's scratching. The

adult flea will remain on the host for the duration of its life unless forcibly removed.

TREATING THE ENVIRONMENT AND THE DOG

Treating fleas should be a two-pronged attack. First, the environment needs to be treated; this includes carpets and furniture, especially the dog's bedding and areas underneath furniture. The environment should be treated with a household spray containing an Insect Growth Regulator (IGR) and an insecticide to kill the adult fleas. Most IGRs are effective against eggs and larvae; they actually mimic the fleas' own hormones and stop the eggs and larvae from developing into adult fleas. There are currently no treatments available to attack the pupa stage of the life cycle, so the adult insecticide is used to kill the newly hatched adult fleas before they find a host. Most IGRs are active for many months, while

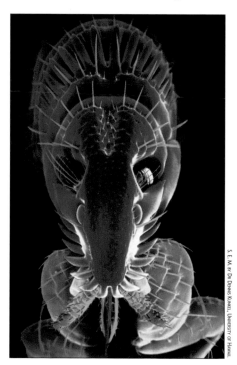

A scanning electron micrograph of a dog or cat flea, *Ctenocephalides*, magnified more than 100x. This image has been colorized for effect.

THE LIFE CYCLE OF THE FLEA

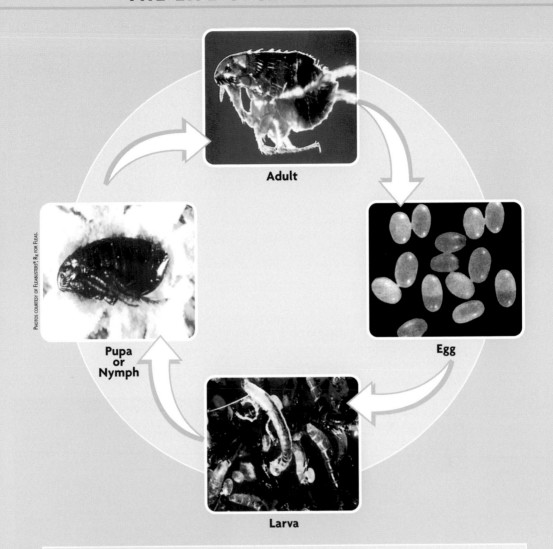

Adult

Egg

Larva

Pupa
or
Nymph

PHOTOS COURTESY OF FLEABUSTERS® RX FOR FLEAS.

A LOOK AT FLEAS
Fleas have been around for millions of years and have adapted to changing host animals. They are able to go through a complete life cycle in less than one month or they can extend their lives to almost two years by remaining as pupae or cocoons. They do not need blood or any other food for up to 20 months.

INSECT GROWTH REGULATOR (IGR)

Two types of products should be used when treating fleas—a product to treat the pet and a product to treat the home. Adult fleas represent less than 1% of the flea population. The pre-adult fleas (eggs, larvae and pupae) represent more than 99% of the flea population and are found in the environment; it is in the case of pre-adult fleas that products containing an Insect Growth Regulator (IGR) should be used in the home.

IGRs are a new class of compounds used to prevent the development of insects. They do not kill the insect outright, but instead use the insect's biology against it to stop it from completing its growth. Products that contain methoprene are the world's first and leading IGRs. Used to control fleas and other insects, this type of IGR will stop flea larvae from developing and protect the house for up to seven months.

The American dog tick, *Dermacentor variabilis*, is probably the most common tick found on dogs. Look at the strength in its eight legs! No wonder it's hard to detach them.

adult insecticides are only active for a few days.

When treating with a household spray, it is a good idea to vacuum before applying the product. This stimulates as many pupae as possible to hatch into adult fleas. The vacuum cleaner should also be treated with an insecticide to prevent the eggs and larvae that have been collected in the vacuum bag from hatching.

The second stage of treatment is to apply an adult insecticide to the dog. Traditionally, this would be in the form of a collar or a spray, but more recent innovations include digestible insecticides that poison the fleas when they ingest the dog's blood. Alternatively, there are drops that, when placed on the back of the dog's neck, spread throughout the dog's hair and skin to kill adult fleas.

TICKS

Though not as common as fleas, ticks are found all over the tropical and temperate world. They don't bite, like fleas; they harpoon. They dig their sharp proboscis (nose) into the dog's skin and drink the blood. Their

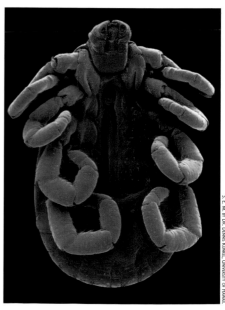

S.E.M. BY DR. DENNIS KUNKEL, UNIVERSITY OF HAWAII

only food and drink is dog's blood. Dogs can get Lyme disease, Rocky Mountain spotted fever, tick bite paralysis and many other diseases from ticks. They may live where fleas are found and they like to hide in cracks or seams in walls. They are controlled the same way fleas are controlled.

The American dog tick, *Dermacentor variabilis*, may well be the most common dog tick in many geographical areas, especially those areas where the climate is hot and humid. Most dog ticks have life expectancies of a week to six months, depending upon climatic conditions. They can neither jump nor fly, but they can crawl slowly and can range up to 16 feet to reach a sleeping or unsuspecting dog.

MITES

Just as fleas and ticks can be problematic for your dog, mites can also lead to an itchy nuisance. Microscopic in size, mites are related to ticks and generally take up permanent residence on their host animal— in this case, your dog! The term *mange* refers to any infestation caused by one of the mighty mites, of which there are six varieties that concern dog owners.

Demodex mites cause a condition known as demodicosis

DEER-TICK CROSSING
The great outdoors may be fun for your dog, but it also is home to dangerous ticks. Deer ticks carry a bacterium known as *Borrelia burgdorferi* and are most active in the autumn and spring. When infections are caught early, penicillin and tetracycline are effective antibiotics, but, if left untreated, the bacteria may cause neurological, kidney and cardiac problems as well as long-term trouble with walking and painful joints.

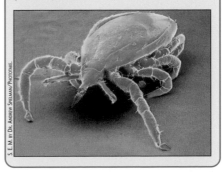

S.E.M. BY DR. ANDREW SPIELMAN/PHOTOTAKE.

PHOTO BY DR. DENNIS KUNKEL, UNIVERSITY OF HAWAII.

The head of an American dog tick, *Dermacentor variabilis*, enlarged and colorized for effect.

The mange mite, *Psoroptes bovis,* can infest cattle and other domestic animals.

Photo by James Hayden/Yoav/Phototake.

Human lice look like dog lice; the two are closely related.

Photo by Dwight R. Kuhn.

(sometimes called red mange or follicular mange), in which the mites live in the dog's hair follicles and sebaceous glands in larger-than-normal amounts. This type of mange is commonly passed from the dam to her puppies and usually shows up on the puppies' muzzles, though demodicosis is not transferable from one normal dog to another. Most dogs recover from this type of mange without any treatment, though topical therapies are commonly prescribed by the vet.

The *Cheyletiellosis* mite is the hook-mouthed culprit associated with "walking dandruff," a condition that affects dogs as well as cats and rabbits. This mite lives on the surface of the animal's skin and is readily transferable through direct or indirect contact with an affected animal. The dandruff is present in the form of scaly skin, which may or may not be itchy. If not treated, this mange can affect a whole kennel of dogs and can be spread to humans as well.

The *Sarcoptes* mite causes intense itching on the dog in the form of a condition known as scabies or sarcoptic mange. The cycle of the *Sarcoptes* mite lasts about three weeks, and the mites live in the top layer of the dog's skin (epidermis), preferably in areas with little hair. Scabies is highly contagious and can be passed to humans. Sometimes an allergic reaction to the mite worsens the severe itching associated with sarcoptic mange.

Ear mites, *Otodectes cynotis,* lead to otodectic mange, which most commonly affects the outer ear canal of the dog, though other areas can be affected as well. Dogs with ear-mite infestation commonly scratch at their ears, causing further irritation, and shake their heads. Dark brown droppings in the outer ear confirm the diagnosis. Your vet can prescribe a treatment to flush out the ears and kill any eggs in the ears. A complete month of treatment is necessary to cure the mange.

Two other mites, less common in dogs, include *Dermanyssus gallinae* (the poultry or red mite) and *Eutrombicula alfreddugesi* (the North American mite associated with trombiculidiasis or chigger infestation). The poultry mite frequently lives on chickens, but can transfer to dogs who spend time near farm animals. Chigger infestation affects dogs in the

> **DO NOT MIX**
> Never mix parasite-control products without first consulting your vet. Some products can become toxic when combined with others and can cause fatal consequences.

> **NOT A DROP TO DRINK**
> Never allow your dog to swim in polluted water or public areas where water quality can be suspect. Even perfectly clear water can harbor parasites, many of which can cause serious to fatal illnesses in canines. Areas inhabited by waterfowl and other wildlife are especially dangerous.

central US who have exposure to woodlands. The types of mange caused by both of these mites are treatable by veterinarians.

INTERNAL PARASITES

Most animals—fishes, birds and mammals, including dogs and humans—have worms and other parasites that live inside their bodies. According to Dr. Herbert R. Axelrod, the fish pathologist, there are two kinds of parasites: dumb and smart. The smart parasites live in peaceful cooperation with their hosts (symbiosis), while the dumb parasites kill their hosts. Most worm infections are relatively easy to control. If they are not controlled, they weaken the host dog to the point that other medical problems occur, but they do not kill the host as dumb parasites would.

A brown dog tick, *Rhipicephalus sanguineus*, is an uncommon but annoying tick found on dogs.

PHOTO BY CAROLINA BIOLOGICAL SUPPLY/PHOTOTAKE.

The roundworm *Rhabditis* can infect both dogs and humans.

The roundworm, *Ascaris lumbricoides*.

ROUNDWORMS

Average-size dogs can pass 1,360,000 roundworm eggs every day. For example, if there were only 1 million dogs in the world, the world would be saturated with thousands of tons of dog feces. These feces would contain around 15,000,000,000 roundworm eggs.

Up to 31% of home yards and children's sand boxes in the US contain roundworm eggs.

Flushing dog's feces down the toilet is not a safe practice because the usual sewage treatments do not destroy roundworm eggs.

Infected puppies start shedding roundworm eggs at three weeks of age. They can be infected by their mother's milk.

ROUNDWORMS

The roundworms that infect dogs are known scientifically as *Toxocara canis*. They live in the dog's intestines and shed eggs continually. It has been estimated that a dog produces about 6 or more ounces of feces every day. Each ounce of feces averages hundreds of thousands of roundworm eggs. There are no known areas in which dogs roam that do not contain roundworm eggs. The greatest danger of roundworms is that they infect people, too! It is wise to have your dog tested regularly for roundworms.

In young puppies, roundworms cause bloated bellies, diarrhea, coughing and vomiting, and are transmitted from the dam (through blood or milk). Affected puppies will not appear as animated as normal puppies. The worms appear spaghetti-like, measuring as long as 6 inches. Adult dogs can acquire roundworms through coprophagia (eating contaminated feces) or by killing rodents that carry roundworms.

Roundworm infection can kill puppies and cause severe problems in adults, as the hatched larvae travel to the lungs and trachea through the bloodstream. Cleanliness is the best preventative for roundworms. Always pick up after your dog and dispose of feces in appropriate receptacles.

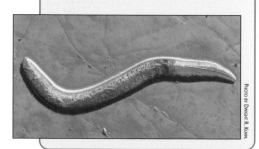

PHOTO BY DWIGHT R. KUHN.

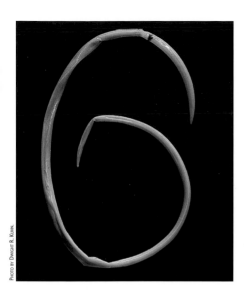

Photo by Dwight R. Kuhn.

Hookworms

In the United States, dog owners have to be concerned about four different species of hookworm, the most common and most serious of which is *Ancylostoma caninum,* which prefers warm climates. The others are *Ancylostoma braziliense, Ancylostoma tubaeforme* and *Uncinaria stenocephala,* the latter of which is a concern to dogs living in the northern US and Canada, as this species prefers cold climates. Hookworms are dangerous to humans as well as to dogs and cats, and can be the cause of severe anemia due to iron deficiency. The worm uses its teeth to attach itself to the dog's intestines and changes the site of its attachment about six times per day. Each time the worm repositions itself, the dog loses

blood and can become anemic. *Ancylostoma caninum* is the most likely of the four species to cause anemia in the dog.

Symptoms of hookworm infection include dark stools, weight loss, general weakness, pale coloration and anemia, as well as possible skin problems. Fortunately, hookworms are easily purged from the affected dog with a number of medications that have proven effective. Discuss these with your veterinarian. Most heartworm preventatives include a hookworm insecticide as well.

Owners also must be aware that hookworms can infect humans, who can acquire the larvae through exposure to contaminated feces. Since the worms cannot complete their life cycle on a human, the worms simply infest the skin and cause irritation. This condition is known as cutaneous larva migrans syndrome. As a preventative, use disposable gloves or a "poop-scoop" to pick up your dog's droppings and prevent your dog (or neighborhood cats) from defecating in children's play areas.

The hookworm, *Ancylostoma caninum.*

Photo by C. James Webb/Phototake.

The infective stage of the hookworm larva.

TAPEWORMS

Humans, rats, squirrels, foxes, coyotes, wolves and domestic dogs are all susceptible to tapeworm infection. Except in humans, tapeworms are usually not a fatal infection. Infected individuals can harbor 1000 parasitic worms.

Tapeworms, like some other types of worm, are hermaphroditic, meaning male and female in the same worm.

If dogs eat infected rats or mice, or anything else infected with tapeworm, they get the tapeworm disease. One month after attaching to a dog's intestine, the worm starts shedding eggs. These eggs are infective immediately. Infective eggs can live for a few months without a host animal.

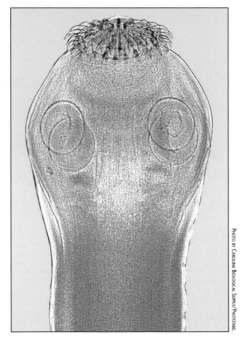

The head and rostellum (the round prominence on the scolex) of a tapeworm, which infects dogs and humans.

PHOTO BY CAROLINA BIOLOGICAL SUPPLY/PHOTOTAKE.

TAPEWORMS

There are many species of tapeworm, all of which are carried by fleas! The most common tapeworm affecting dogs is known as *Dipylidium caninum*. The dog eats the flea and starts the tapeworm cycle. Humans can also be infected with tapeworms—so don't eat fleas! Fleas are so small that your dog could pass them onto your hands, your plate or your food and thus make it possible for you to ingest a flea that is carrying tapeworm eggs.

While tapeworm infection is not life-threatening in dogs (smart parasite!), it can be the cause of a very serious liver disease for humans. About 50% of the humans infected with *Echinococcus multilocularis*, a type of tapeworm that causes alveolar hydatid, perish.

WHIPWORMS

In North America, whipworms are counted among the most common parasitic worms in dogs. The whipworm's scientific name is *Trichuris vulpis*. These worms attach themselves in the lower parts of the intestine, where they feed. Affected dogs may only experience upset tummies, colic and diarrhea. These worms, however, can live for months or years in the dog, beginning their larval stage in the small intestine, spending their adult stage in the large intestine and finally passing infective eggs through the dog's feces. The only way to detect whipworms is through a fecal examination, though this is not always foolproof. Treatment for whipworms is tricky, due to the worms' unusual life-cycle pattern, and very often dogs are reinfected due to exposure to infective eggs on the ground. The whipworm eggs can survive in the environment for as long as five years; thus, cleaning up droppings in your own backyard as well as in public places is absolutely essential for sanitation purposes and the health of your dog and others.

THREADWORMS

Though less common than round-worms, hookworms and those previously mentioned, thread-

worms concern dog owners in the southwestern US and Gulf Coast area, where the climate is hot and humid. Living in the small intestine of the dog, this worm measures a mere 2 millimeters and is round in shape. Like that of the whipworm, the threadworm's life cycle is very complex and the eggs and larvae are passed through the feces. A deadly disease in humans, *Strongyloides* readily infects people, and the handling of feces is the most common means of transmission. Threadworms are most often seen in young puppies; bloody diarrhea and pneumonia are symptoms. Sick puppies must be isolated and treated immediately; vets recom-mend a follow-up treatment one month later.

HEARTWORM PREVENTATIVES

There are many heartworm preventatives on the market, many of which are sold at your veterinarian's office. These products can be given daily or monthly, depending on the manufacturer's instructions. All of these preventatives contain chemical insecticides directed at killing heartworms, which leads to some controversy among dog owners. In effect, heartworm preventatives are neces-sary evils, though you should determine how necessary based on your pet's lifestyle. There is no doubt that heartworm is a dreadful disease that threatens the lives of dogs. However, the likelihood of your dog's being bitten by an infected mosquito is slim in most places, and a mosquito-repellent (or an herbal remedy such as Wormwood or

Black Walnut) is much safer for your dog and will not compromise his immune system (the way heartworm preventatives will). Should you decide to use the tradi-tional preventative "medications," you can consider giving the pill every other or third month. Since the toxins in the pill will kill the heartworms at all stages of develop-ment, the pill would be effective in killing larvae, nymphs or adults and it takes four months for the larvae to reach the adult stage. Thus, there is no rationale to poison-ing the dog's system on a monthly basis. Lastly, do not give the pill during the winter months since there are no mosquitoes around to pass on their infection, unless you live in a tropical environment.

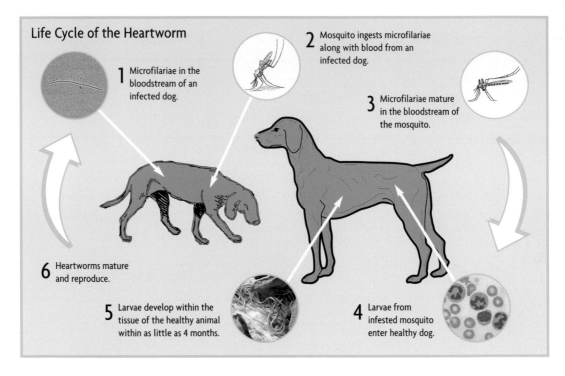

Life Cycle of the Heartworm

1 Microfilariae in the bloodstream of an infected dog.

2 Mosquito ingests microfilariae along with blood from an infected dog.

3 Microfilariae mature in the bloodstream of the mosquito.

4 Larvae from infested mosquito enter healthy dog.

5 Larvae develop within the tissue of the healthy animal within as little as 4 months.

6 Heartworms mature and reproduce.

HEARTWORMS

Heartworms are thin, extended worms up to 12 inches long, which live in a dog's heart and the major blood vessels surrounding it. Dogs may have up to 200 worms. Symptoms may be loss of energy, loss of appetite, coughing, the development of a pot belly and anemia.

Heartworms are transmitted by mosquitoes. The mosquito drinks the blood of an infected dog and takes in larvae with the blood. The larvae, called microfilariae, develop within the body of the mosquito and are passed on to the next dog bitten after the larvae mature. It takes two to three weeks for the larvae to develop to the infective stage within the body of the mosquito. Dogs are usually treated at about six weeks of age and maintained on a prophylactic dose given monthly.

Blood testing for heartworms is not necessarily indicative of how seriously your dog is infected. Although this is a dangerous disease, it is not easy for a dog to be infected. Discuss the various preventatives with your vet, as there are many different types now available. Together you can decide on a safe course of prevention for your dog.

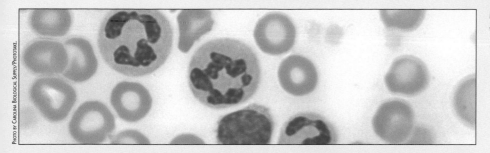

Photo by Carolina Biological Supply/Phototake.

Magnified heart-worm larvae, *Diro-filaria immitis.*

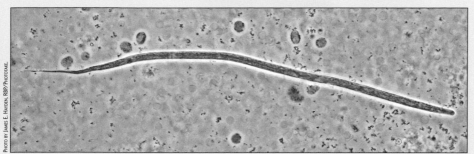

Photo by James E. Hayden, RBP/Phototake.

Heartworm, *Diro-filaria immitis.*

Photo by James E. Hayden, RPB/Phototake.

The heart of a dog infected with canine heart-worm, *Dirofilaria immitis.*

HOMEOPATHY:
an alternative
to conventional
medicine

"Less is Most"

Using this principle, the strength of a homeopathic remedy is measured by the number of serial dilutions that were undertaken to create it. The greater the number of serial dilutions, the greater the strength of the homeopathic remedy. The potency of a remedy that has been made by making a dilution of 1 part in 100 parts (or 1/100) is 1c or 1cH. If this remedy is subjected to a series of further dilutions, each one being 1/100, a more dilute and stronger remedy is produced. If the remedy is diluted in this way six times, it is called 6c or 6cH. A dilution of 6c is 1 part in 1,000,000,000,000. In general, higher potencies in more frequent doses are better for acute symptoms and lower potencies in more infrequent doses are more useful for chronic, long-standing problems.

CURING OUR DOGS NATURALLY

Holistic medicine means treating the whole animal as a unique, perfect, living being. Generally, holistic treatments do not suppress the symptoms that the body naturally produces, as do most medications prescribed by conventional doctors and vets. Holistic methods seek to cure disease by regaining balance and harmony in the patient's environment. Some of these methods include use of nutritional therapy, herbs, flower essences, aromatherapy, acupuncture, massage, chiropractic and, of course, the most popular holistic approach, homeopathy.

Homeopathy is a theory or system of treating illness with small doses of substances which, if administered in larger quantities, would produce the symptoms that the patient already has. This approach is often described as "like cures like." Although modern veterinary medicine is geared toward the "quick fix," homeopathy relies on the belief that, given the time, the body is able to heal itself and return to its natural, healthy state.

Choosing a remedy to cure a problem in our dogs is the difficult part of homeopathy. Consult with your vet for a professional diagnosis of your dog's symptoms. Often these symptoms require immediate conventional care. If your vet is willing and knowledgeable, you may attempt a homeopathic remedy. Be aware that cortisone prevents homeopathic remedies from working. There are hundreds of possibilities and combinations to cure many problems in dogs, from basic physical problems such as excessive shedding, fleas or other parasites, unattractive doggy odor, bad breath, upset tummy, obesity, dry, oily or dull coat, diarrhea, ear problems or eye discharge (including tears and dry or mucousy matter), to behavioral abnormalities such as fear of loud noises, habitual licking, poor appetite, excessive barking and various phobias. From alumina to zincum metallicum, the remedies span the planet and the imagination…from flowers and weeds to chemicals, insect droppings, diesel smoke and volcanic ash.

Using "Like to Treat Like"

Unlike conventional medicines that suppress symptoms, homeopathic remedies treat illnesses with small doses of substances that, if administered in larger quantities, would produce the symptoms that the patient already has. While the same homeopathic remedy can be used to treat different symptoms in different dogs, here are some interesting remedies and their uses.

Apis Mellifica
(made from honey bee venom) can be used for allergies or to reduce swelling that occurs in acutely infected kidneys.

Diesel Smoke
can be used to help control travel sickness.

Calcarea Fluorica
(made from calcium fluoride, which helps harden bone structure) can be useful in treating hard lumps in tissues.

Natrum Muriaticum
(made from common salt, sodium chloride) is useful in treating thin, thirsty dogs.

Nitricum Acidum
(made from nitric acid) is used for symptoms you would expect to see from contact with acids, such as lesions, especially where the skin joins the linings of body orifices or openings such as the lips and nostrils.

Symphytum
(made from the herb Knitbone, *Symphytum officianale*) is used to encourage bones to heal.

Urtica Urens
(made from the common stinging nettle) is used in treating painful, irritating rashes.

First Aid at a Glance

Burns
Place the affected area under cool water; use ice if only a small area is burnt.

Bee stings/Insect bites
Apply ice to relieve swelling; antihistamine dosed properly.

Animal bites
Clean any bleeding area; apply pressure until bleeding subsides; go to the vet.

Spider bites
Use cold compress and a pressurized pack to inhibit venom's spreading.

Antifreeze poisoning
Induce vomiting with hydrogen peroxide. Seek *immediate* veterinary help!

Fish hooks
Removal best handled by vet; hook must be cut in order to remove.

Snake bites
Pack ice around bite; contact vet quickly; identify snake for proper antivenin.

Car accident
Move dog from roadway with blanket; seek veterinary aid.

Shock
Calm the dog; keep him warm; seek immediate veterinary help.

Nosebleed
Apply cold compress to the nose; apply pressure to any visible abrasion.

Bleeding
Apply pressure above the area; treat wound by applying a cotton pack.

Heat stroke
Submerge dog in cold bath; cool down with fresh air and water; go to the vet.

Frostbite/Hypothermia
Warm the dog with a warm bath, electric blankets or hot water bottles.

Abrasions
Clean the wound and wash out thoroughly with fresh water; apply antiseptic.

 Remember: an injured dog may attempt to bite a helping hand from fear and confusion. Always muzzle the dog before trying to offer assistance.

Recognizing a Sick Dog

Unlike colicky babies and cranky children, our canine kids cannot tell us when they are feeling ill. Therefore, there are a number of signs that owners can identify to know that their dogs are not feeling well.

Take note for physical manifestations such as:

- unusual, bad odor, including bad breath
- excessive shedding
- wax in the ears, chronic ear irritation
- oily, flaky, dull haircoat
- mucus, tearing or similar discharge in the eyes
- fleas or mites
- mucus in stool, diarrhea
- sensitivity to petting or handling
- licking at paws, scratching face, etc.

Keep an eye out for behavioral changes as well including:

- lethargy, idleness
- lack of patience or general irritability
- lack of interest in food
- phobias (fear of people, loud noises, etc.)
- strange behavior, suspicion, fear
- coprophagia
- more frequent barking
- whimpering, crying

Get Well Soon

You don't need a DVM to provide good TLC to your sick or recovering dog, but you do need to pay attention to some details that normally wouldn't bother him. The following tips will aid Fido's recovery and get him back on his paws again:

- Keep his space free of irritating smells, like heavy perfumes and air fresheners.
- Rest is the best medicine! Avoid harsh lighting that will prevent your dog from sleeping. Shade him from bright sunlight during the day and dim the lights in the evening.
- Keep the noise level down. Animals are more sensitive to sound when they are sick.

- Be attentive to any necessary temperature adjustments. A dog with a fever needs a cool room and cold liquids. A bitch that is whelping or recovering from surgery will be more comfortable in a warm room, consuming warm liquids and food.
- You wouldn't send a sick child back to school early, so don't rush your dog back into a full routine until he seems absolutely ready.

CDS: COGNITIVE DYSFUNCTION SYNDROME
"Old-Dog Syndrome"

There are many ways for you to evaluate old-dog syndrome. Veterinarians have defined CDS (cognitive dysfunction syndrome) as the gradual deterioration of cognitive abilities. These are indicated by changes in the dog's behavior. When a dog changes his routine response, and maladies have been eliminated as the cause of these behavioral changes, then CDS is the usual diagnosis.

More than half the dogs over eight years old suffer from some form of CDS. The older the dog, the more chance he has of suffering from CDS. In humans, doctors often dismiss the CDS behavioral changes as part of "winding down."

There are four major signs of CDS: frequent potty accidents inside the home, sleeping much more or much less than normal, acting confused and failing to respond to social stimuli.

SYMPTOMS OF CDS

FREQUENT POTTY ACCIDENTS
- *Urinates in the house.*
- *Defecates in the house.*
- *Doesn't signal that he wants to go out.*

SLEEP PATTERNS
- *Awakens more slowly.*
- *Sleeps more than normal during the day.*
- *Sleeps less during the night.*

CONFUSION
- *Goes outside and just stands there.*
- *Appears confused with a faraway look in his eyes.*
- *Hides more often.*
- *Doesn't recognize friends.*
- *Doesn't come when called.*
- *Walks around listlessly and without a destination.*

FAILURE TO RESPOND TO SOCIAL STIMULI
- *Comes to people less frequently, whether called or not.*
- *Doesn't tolerate petting for more than a short time.*
- *Doesn't come to the door when you return home.*

BERNESE MOUNTAIN DOG

The term *old* is a qualitative term. For dogs, as well as their masters, old is relative. Certainly we can all distinguish between a puppy Bernese and an adult Bernese—there are the obvious physical traits, such as size, appearance and facial expressions, and personality traits. Puppies and young dogs like to play with children. Children's natural exuberance is a good match for the seemingly endless energy of young dogs. They like to run, jump, chase and retrieve. When dogs grow older and cease their interaction with children, they are often thought of as being too old to play with the kids.

On the other hand, if a Bernese is only exposed to people who lead quieter lifestyles, his life will normally be less active and he will not seem to be getting old as his activity level slows down.

If people live to be 100 years old, dogs live to be 20 years old. While this is a good rule of thumb, it is very inaccurate. When trying to compare dog years to human years, you cannot make a generalization about all dogs. You can make the generalization that eight years is a good lifespan

for a Bernese, which is not terribly long compared to the life expectancies of many other breeds and reminds us how precious our time with our beloved Berner truly is. Although some Berners can live to ten or better, the prevalence of cancer in the breed threatens the life of every dog.

WHAT TO LOOK FOR IN SENIORS

Depending on the individual dog, his activity level and his lifestyle, a Berner can be considered a senior by the time his is five to seven years of age. The term *senior* does not imply that the dog is geriatric and has begun to fail

GETTING OLD
The bottom line is simply that a dog is getting old when you think he is getting old because he slows down in his general activities, including walking, running, eating, jumping and retrieving. On the other hand, certain activities increase, like more sleeping, more barking and more repetition of habits like going to the door when you put your coat on without being called.

SIGNS OF AGING

An old dog starts to show one or more of the following symptoms:

- Sleep patterns are deeper and longer and the old dog is harder to awaken.

- Food intake diminishes.

- Responses to calls, whistles and other signals are ignored more and more.

- Eye contacts do not evoke tail wagging (assuming they once did).

- The hair on his face and paws starts to turn gray. The color breakdown usually starts around the eyes and mouth.

in mind and body. Aging is essentially a slowing process. Humans readily admit that they feel a difference in their activity level from age 20 to 30, and then from 30 to 40, etc. By treating the six- or seven-year-old dog as a senior, owners are able to implement certain therapeutic and preventative medical strategies with the help of their veterinarians. A senior-care program should include at least two veterinary visits per year, screening sessions to determine the dog's health status, as well as nutritional counseling. Veterinarians determine the senior dog's health status through a blood smear for a complete blood count, serum

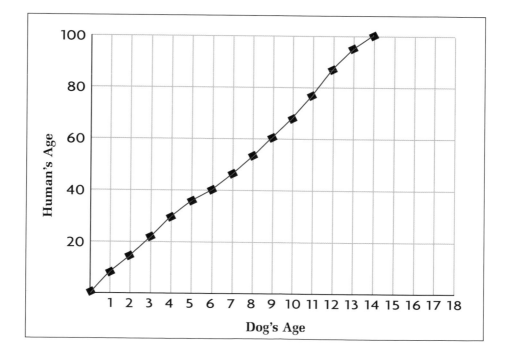

chemistry profile with electrolytes, urinalysis, blood pressure check, electrocardiogram, ocular tonometry (pressure on the eyeball) and dental prophylaxis.

Such an extensive program for senior dogs is well advised before owners start to see the obvious physical signs of aging, such as slower and inhibited movement, graying, increased sleep/nap periods and disinterest in play and other activity. This preventative program promises a longer, healthier life for the aging dog. Among the physical problems common in aging dogs are the loss of sight and hearing, arthritis, kidney and liver failure, diabetes mellitus, heart disease and Cushing's disease (a hormonal disease).

In addition to the physical manifestations discussed, there are some behavioral changes and problems related to aging dogs. Dogs suffering from hearing or vision loss, dental discomfort or arthritis can become aggressive. Likewise the near-deaf and/or blind dog may be startled more easily and react in an unexpectedly aggressive manner. Seniors suffering from senility can become more impatient and irritable. Housesoiling accidents are associated with loss of mobility, kidney problems and loss of sphincter control as well as plaque accumulation, physiological brain changes and reactions to medications. Older dogs, just like young

HORMONAL PROBLEMS

Although graying is normal and expected in older dogs, a flaky coat or loss of hair is not. Such coat problems may point to a hormonal problem. Hypothyroidism, in which the thyroid gland fails to produce the normal amount of hormones, is one such problem. Your veterinarian can treat hypothyroidism with an oral supplement. The condition is more common in certain breeds, so discuss its likelihood in your dog with your breeder and vet.

puppies, suffer from separation anxiety, which can lead to excessive barking, whining, housesoiling and destructive behavior. Seniors may become fearful of

NOTICING THE SYMPTOMS

The symptoms listed below are symptoms that gradually appear and become more noticeable. They are not life-threatening; however, the symptoms below are to be taken very seriously and warrant a discussion with your veterinarian:

- Your dog cries and whimpers when he moves, and he stops running completely.
- Convulsions start or become more serious and frequent. The usual convulsion (spasm) is when the dog stiffens and starts to tremble, being unable or unwilling to move. The seizure usually lasts for 5 to 30 minutes.
- Your dog drinks more water and urinates more frequently. Wetting and bowel accidents take place indoors without warning.
- Vomiting becomes more and more frequent.

everyday sounds, such as vacuum cleaners, heaters, thunder and passing traffic. Some dogs have difficulty sleeping, due to discomfort, the need for frequent toilet visits and the like.

Owners should avoid spoiling the older dog with fatty treats. Obesity is a common problem in older dogs and subtracts years from their lives. Keep the senior dog as trim as possible since excessive weight puts additional stress on the body's vital organs. Some breeders recommend supplementing the diet with foods high in fiber and lower in calories. Adding fresh vegetables and marrow broth to the senior's diet makes a tasty, low-calorie, low-fat supplement. Vets also offer specialty diets for senior dogs that are worth exploring.

Your dog, as he nears his twilight years, needs his owner's patience and good care more than ever. Never punish an older dog for an accident or abnormal behavior. For all the years of love, protection and companionship that your dog has provided, he deserves special attention and courtesies. The older dog may need to relieve himself at 3 a.m. because he can no longer hold it for eight hours. Older dogs may not be able to remain crated for more than two or three hours. It may be time to give up a sofa or chair to your old friend. Although he may not seem as enthusiastic about your attention and petting, he does appreciate the considerations you offer as he gets older.

Your Berner does not understand why his world is slowing down. Owners must make the transition into the golden years as pleasant and rewarding as possible.

WHAT TO DO WHEN THE TIME COMES

You are never fully prepared to make a rational decision about putting your dog to sleep. It is very obvious that you love your Bernese Mountain Dog or you would not be reading this book. Putting a loved dog to sleep is extremely difficult. It is a decision that must be made with your veterinarian. You are usually forced to make the decision when one of the life-threatening symptoms listed above becomes serious enough for you to seek veterinary help. If the prognosis of the malady indicates the end is near and your beloved pet will only suffer more and experience no enjoyment for the balance of his life, then euthanasia is the right choice.

WHAT IS EUTHANASIA?

Euthanasia derives from the Greek, meaning *good death*. In other words, it means the planned, painless killing of a dog suffering from a painful, incurable condition, or who is so aged that

AN ANCIENT ACHE

As ancient a disease as any, arthritis remains poorly explained for human and dog alike. Fossils dating back 100 million years show the deterioration caused by arthritis. Human fossils two million years old show the disease in man. The most common type of arthritis affecting dogs is known as osteoarthritis, which occurs in adult dogs before their senior years. Obesity aggravating the dog's joints has been cited as a factor in arthritis.

The Bernese is known to suffer from inflamed joints caused by an auto-immune disease called immune-mediated polyarthritis (IMPA). The cause of IMPA is not known, though it occurs more frequently in bitches as early as 18 months of age. Rheumatoid disease destroys joint cartilage and causes arthritic joints. Pituitary dysfunctions as well as diabetes have been associated with arthritis. Veterinarians treat arthritis variously, including aspirin, "bed rest" in the dog's crate, physical therapy and exercise, heat therapy (with a heating pad), providing soft bedding materials and treatment with corticosteroids (to reduce pain and swelling temporarily). Your vet will be able to recommend a course of action to help relieve your arthritic pal.

New drugs on the market promise relief for our four-legged pal's aches and pains. Ask your vet about which products he recommends.

he cannot walk, see, eat or control his excretory functions.

Euthanasia is usually accomplished by injection with an overdose of an anesthesia or barbiturate. Aside from the prick of the needle, the experience is usually painless.

MAKING THE DECISION

The decision to euthanize your dog is never easy. The days during which the dog becomes ill and the end occurs can be unusually stressful for you. If this is your first experience with the death of a loved one, you may need the comfort dictated by your religious beliefs. If you are the head of the family and have children, you should have involved them in the decision of putting your Bernese to sleep. Usually your dog can be maintained on drugs for a few days in order to give you ample time to make a decision. During this time, talking with members of your family or even people who have lived through this same experience can ease the burden of your inevitable decision.

THE FINAL RESTING PLACE

Dogs can have some of the same privileges as humans. The remains of your beloved dog can be buried in a pet cemetery, which is generally expensive. Dogs who have died at home can be buried in your yard in a place suitably marked with some stone

Some Bernese owners choose to memorialize their beloved dogs in pet cemeteries.

Bernese Mountain Dog or perhaps a different breed so as to avoid comparison with your beloved friend? Most people usually choose the same breed because they know and love the characteristics of that breed. Then, too, they often know people who have the same breed and perhaps they are lucky enough that one of their friends expects a litter soon. What could be better?

Most pet cemeteries have facilities for storing dogs' ashes.

or newly planted tree or bush. Alternatively, they can be cremated individually and the ashes returned to you. A less expensive option is mass cremation, although, of course, the ashes can not then be returned. Vets can usually arrange the cremation on your behalf. The cost of these options should always be discussed frankly and openly with your veterinarian.

GETTING ANOTHER DOG?

The grief of losing your beloved dog will be as lasting as the grief of losing a human friend or relative. In most cases, if your dog died of old age (if there is such a thing), he had slowed down considerably. Do you want a new Bernese puppy to replace it? Or are you better off finding a more mature Berner, say two to three years of age, which will usually be house-trained and will have an already developed personality? In this case, you can find out if you like each other after a few hours of being together.

The decision is, of course, your own. Do you want another

> **KEEPING SENIORS WARM**
> The coats of many older dogs become thinner as they age, which makes them more sensitive to cold temperatures and more susceptible to illness. During cold weather, limit time spent outdoors and be extremely cautious with any artificial sources of warmth such as heat lamps, as these can cause severe burns. Your old-timer may need a sweater to wear over his coat.

SHOWING YOUR
BERNESE MOUNTAIN DOG

If you purchased a Berner puppy with definite plans to show him, then you will have informed the breeder of your intentions. Not every Berner puppy will grow up to be a show-dog candidate, so the breeder's input and advice are critical to your potential success in conformation showing. To the novice, exhibiting a Berner in the show ring may look easy, but it takes a lot of hard work and devotion to do top winning at a show such as the prestigious Westminster Kennel Club, not to mention a little luck too!

The first concept that the canine novice learns when watching a dog show is that each dog first competes against members of its own breed. Once the judge has selected the best member of each breed (Best of Breed), provided that the show is judged on a Group system, that chosen dog will compete with other dogs in its group. The Berner competes in the Working Group. Finally, the dogs chosen first in each group will compete for Best in Show.

The second concept that you must understand is that the dogs are not actually compared against one another. The judge compares each dog against its breed standard. While some early breed standards were indeed based on specific dogs that were famous or popular, many dedicated enthusiasts say that a perfect specimen, as described in the standard, has never walked into a show ring, has never been bred and, to the woe of dog breeders around the globe, does not exist. Breeders attempt to get as close to this ideal as possible with every litter, but theoretically the "perfect" dog is so elusive that it is impossible.

If you are interested in exploring the world of dog showing, your best bet is to join your local breed club or the national parent club, which is the Bernese Mountain Dog Club of America, Inc. (BMDCA). The BMDCA and local clubs host specialty shows in which only Berners can compete. The national specialty is held by

AKC GROUPS
For showing purposes, the American Kennel Club divides its recognized breeds into seven groups: Sporting Dogs, Hounds, Working Dogs, Terriers, Toys, Non-Sporting Dogs and Herding Dogs.

the BMDCA annually and changes its location each year. Specialties are exciting for fanciers and fans alike, as they include not only conformation classes but also drafting, tracking and more! Clubs also send out newsletters, and some organize training days and seminars in order that people may learn more about their chosen breed. To locate the breed club closest to you, contact the American Kennel Club, which furnishes the rules and regulations for many of these events plus general dog registration and other basic requirements of dog ownership.

If your Berner is of age and registered, you can enter him in a dog show where the breed is offered classes. Only unaltered dogs can be entered in a dog show, so if you have spayed or neutered your Berner, you cannot compete in conformation shows. The reason for this is simple. Dog shows are the main forum to prove which representatives in a breed are worthy of being bred. Only dogs that have proven themselves in the show ring by attaining a Champion title—the recognized "seal of approval" for excellence in pure-bred dogs—should be bred. Altered dogs, however, can participate in other events such as obedience trials and the Canine Good Citizen program.

Before you actually step into the ring, you would be well advised to sit back and observe

INFORMATION ON CLUBS
You can get information about dog shows from the national kennel clubs:

American Kennel Club
5580 Centerview Dr., Raleigh, NC 27606-3390
www.akc.org

United Kennel Club
100 E. Kilgore Road, Kalamazoo, MI 49002
www.ukcdogs.com

Canadian Kennel Club
89 Skyway Ave., Suite 100, Etobicoke, Ontario M9W 6R4 Canada
www.ckc.ca

The Kennel Club
1-5 Clarges St., Piccadilly, London W1Y 8AB, UK
www.the-kennel-club.org.uk

the judge's ring procedure. If it is your first time in the ring, do not be over-anxious and run to the front of the line. It is much better to stand back and study how the exhibitor in front of you is performing. The judge asks each handler to "stack" the dog, showing the dog off to his best advantage. The judge will observe the dog from a distance and from different angles, and approach the dog to check his teeth, overall structure, alertness and muscle tone, as well as consider how well the dog "conforms" to the standard. Most importantly, the judge will have the exhibitor move the dog around the ring in some pattern that he should specify. Finally, the judge will give the dog one last look before moving on to the next exhibitor.

If you are not in the top four in your class at your first show, do not be discouraged. Be patient and consistent, and you may eventually find yourself in a winning line-up. Remember that the winners were once in your shoes and have devoted many hours and much money to earn the placement. If you find that your dog is losing every time and never getting a nod, you should consider a different dog sport like agility or obedience, or even a carting or weight-pulling event!

SHOW-RING ETIQUETTE

Just as with anything else, there is a certain etiquette to the show ring that can only be learned through experience. Showing your dog can be quite intimidating to you as a novice when it seems as if everyone else knows what he is doing. You can familiarize yourself with ring procedure beforehand by taking showing classes to prepare you and your dog for conformation showing and by talking with experienced handlers. When you are in the ring, it is very important to pay attention and listen to the instructions you are given by the judge about where to move your dog. Remember, even the most skilled handlers had to start somewhere. Keep it up and you too will become a proficient handler as you gain practice and experience.

Keep mind, too, that there is absolutely nothing wrong with your Berner just being your full-time best friend!

OBEDIENCE TRIALS

Obedience trials in the US trace back to the early 1930s when organized obedience training was developed to demonstrate how well dog and owner could work together. The pioneer of obedience trials is Mrs. Helen Whitehouse Walker, a Standard Poodle fancier, who designed a series of exercises after the Associated, Sheep, Police Army Dog Society of Great Britain. Since the days of Mrs. Walker, obedience trials have grown by leaps and bounds, and today there are over 2,000 trials held in the US every year, with more than 100,000 dogs competing. Any AKC-registered dog can enter an obedience trial, regardless of conformational disqualifications or neutering.

Obedience trials are divided into three levels of progressive difficulty. At the first level, the Novice, dogs compete for the title Companion Dog (CD); at the intermediate level, the Open, dogs compete for the title Companion Dog Excellent (CDX); and at the advanced level, dogs compete for the title Utility Dog (UD). Classes are sub-divided into "A" (for beginners) and "B" (for more experienced handlers). A perfect score at any level is 200, and a

BECOMING A CHAMPION

An official AKC champion of record requires that a dog accumulate 15 points under three different judges, including two "majors" under different judges. Points are awarded based on the number of dogs entered into competition, varying from breed to breed and place to place. A win of three, four or five points is considered a "major." The AKC annually assigns a schedule of points to adjust the variations that accompany a breed's popularity and the population of a given area.

dog must score 170 or better to earn a "leg," of which three are needed to earn the title. To earn points, the dog must score more than 50% of the available points in each exercise; the possible points range from 20 to 40.

Each level consists of a different set of exercises. In the Novice level, the dog must heel on- and off-lead, come, long sit, long down and stand for examination. These skills are the basic ones required for a well-behaved "Companion Dog." The Open level requires that the dog

There is nothing more exciting for the proud owner than taking home a ribbon from a dog show!

perform the same exercises above but without a leash for extended lengths of time, as well as retrieve a dumbbell, broad jump and drop on recall. In the Utility level, dogs must perform ten difficult exercises, including scent discrimination, hand signals for basic commands, directed jump and directed retrieve.

Once a dog has earned the UD title, he can compete with other proven obedience dogs for the coveted title of Utility Dog Excellent (UDX), which requires that the dog win "legs" in ten shows. Utility Dogs who earn "legs" in Open B and Utility B earn points toward their Obedience Trial Champion title. In 1977 the title Obedience Trial Champion (OTCh.) was estab-lished by the AKC. To become an OTCh., a dog must earn 100 points, which requires three first places in Open B and Utility under three different judges.

AGILITY TRIALS

Having had its origins in the UK back in 1997, agility had its official AKC beginning in the US in August 1994, when the first licensed agility trials were held. The AKC allows all registered breeds to participate, providing the dog is 12 months of age or older. Agility is designed so that the handler demonstrates how well the dog can work at his side. The handler directs his dog over an obstacle course that includes jumps (such as those used in the

Depending on the show, your Berner could win a cup, a ribbon or a medal in conformation competition.

obedience trials), as well as tires, the dog walk, weave poles, pipe tunnels, collapsed tunnels, etc. While working his way through the course, the dog must keep one eye and ear on the handler and the rest of his body on the course. The handler gives verbal and hand signals to guide the dog through the course.

Agility is great fun for dog and owner with many rewards for everyone involved. Interested owners should join a training club that has obstacles and experienced agility handlers who can introduce you and your dog to the "ropes" (and tires, tunnels, etc.).

TRACKING

Any dog is capable of tracking, using his nose to follow a trail, and the Berner is an exceptional candidate for tracking—he's willingly nosy and able! Tracking tests are exciting and competitive ways to test your Berner's instinctive scenting ability and his ability to search and rescue, a feat that a few brave Berners have had some success. The AKC started tracking tests in 1937, when the first licensed test took place as part of the Utility level at an obedience trial. Ten years later in 1947, the AKC offered the first title, Tracking Dog (TD). It was not until 1980 that the AKC added the title Tracking Dog Excellent (TDX), which was followed by the title Versatile

SHOW QUALITY SHOWS
While you may purchase a puppy in the hope of having a successful career in the show ring, it is impossible to tell, at eight to ten weeks of age, whether your dog will be a contender. Some promising pups end up with minor to serious faults that prevent them from taking home an award, but this certainly does not mean they can't be the best of companions for you and your family. To find out if your potential show dog is show-quality, enter him in a match to see how a judge evaluates him. You may also take him back to your breeder as he matures to see what he might advise.

THE GRAND PRIX OF OBEDIENCE

The American Kennel Club National Obedience Invitational is the Grand Prix or Kentucky Derby for obedience dogs in the US. This wonderful two-day trial began in 1995 and is held annually. Only obedience dogs (Utility Dogs or Obedience Trial Champions) that are ranked in the top 25 in their breed (or the top three of their own breed) are invited to participate. The dogs are ranked based on their OTCh. points. The period of eligibility varies each year but usually covers an 18-month period.

The winner of the National Obedience Invitational earns the prestigious title of National Obedience Champion (NOC). Since the inception of Invitational, the Sporting Dogs have dominated (namely Golden Retrievers), though there has been at least one Herding Dog NOC, a Shetland Sheepdog.

Surface Tracking (VST) in 1995. The title Champion Tracker (CT) is awarded to a dog who has earned all three titles

In the beginning level of tracking, the owner follows the dog through a field on a long lead. To earn the TD title, the dog must follow a track laid by a human 30 to 120 minutes prior. The track is about 500 yards with up to 5 directional changes. The TDX requires that the dog follow a track that is 3 to 5 hours old over a course up to 1,000 yards with up to 7 directional changes. The VST requires that the dog follow a track up to 5 hours old through an urban setting.

HERDING

Most owners do not think of their Berners as "herding dogs," but historically the breed has been used in this capacity as well. The Bernese Mountain Dog is one of the "loose eyed and upright" dogs, along with other multi-purpose farm dogs like the Kerry Blue, Standard Schnauzer and Rottweiler. Berners do not crouch to approach the stock (thus "upright") and do not stare the animals into obeying ("loose-eyed" as opposed to "strong-eyed").

Many owners begin their Berners with instinct tests, which are often sponsored by breed clubs. Experienced handlers are needed to test the dog's reaction to stock. Some Berners will become excited when watching the stock; others will show little interest. Dogs brimming with herding enthusiasm will intensely watch the stock, circle about, move with the sheep or chase it. Before your Berner is a year old, you should introduce him to stock to test his reaction. If he's not turned on by the goats right away, give him another chance in a few months. The more exposure a dog has to stock in his early months, the more lasting will his interest be in the stock as an adult.

While the AKC offers herding tests and trials for all breeds in the Herding Group (as well as the Rottweiler and the Samoyed of the Working Group), the Berner is not eligible. Nonetheless, there are instinct certification tests, which most Berners pass with flying colors. The breed can participate in herding trials sponsored by the American Herding Breed Association (AHBA), as well as the Australian Shepherd Club of America (ASCA). The AHBA, founded in 1986, focuses on practical herding work and is open to many breeds, including the multi-purpose breeds like the Berner. The Herding Trial Program is designed to test dog's herding abilities in trials of varying levels of difficulty (Started, Intermediate and Advanced), plus a farm/ranch course. Dogs can also participate in the Herding Capability Tests, which are similar to instinct tests offered by breed clubs.

CARTING
While the Berner shines in many arenas of the dog sport, of course, carting or drafting are the breed's bred-for purpose. In carting, the Berner has no competition (except other Berners). Sponsored by the Bernese Mountain Dog Club of America, drafting trials require that the Berner demonstrate control of the cart as well as strength and endurance in pulling. The parent club offers four titles in draft work: NDD (Novice Draft Dog), DD (Draft Dog), NBDD

With training and encouragement, the Berner can do anything! This Berner is practicing for an obedience trial in his owner's backyard.

AMERICAN KENNEL CLUB TITLES

The AKC offers over 40 different titles to dogs in competition. Depending on the events that your dog can enter, different titles apply. Some titles can be applied as prefixes, meaning that they are placed before the dog's name (e.g., Ch. King of the Road) and others are used as suffixes, placed after the dog's name (e.g., King of the Road, CD).

These titles are used as prefixes:

Conformation Dog Shows
- Ch. (Champion)

Obedience Trials
- NOC (National Obedience Champion)
- OTCH (Obedience Trial Champion)
- VCCH (Versatile Companion Champion)

Tracking Tests
- CT [Champion Tracker (TD,TDX and VST)]

Agility Trials
- MACH (Master Agility Champion)
- MACH2, MACH3, MACH4, etc.

Field Trials
- FC (Field Champion)
- AFC (Amateur Field Champion)
- NFC (National Field Champion)
- NAFC (National Amateur Field Champion)
- NOGDC (National Open Gun Dog Champion)
- AKC GDSC (AKC Gun Dog Stake Champion)
- AKC RGDSC (AKC Retrieving Gun Dog Stake Champion)

Herding Trials
- HC (Herding Champion)

Dual
- DC (Dual Champion — Ch. and FC)

Triple
- TC (Triple Champion — Ch., FC and OTCH)

Coonhounds
- NCH (Nite Champion)
- GNCH (Grand Nite Champion)
- SHNCH (Senior Grand Nite Champion)
- GCH (Senior Champion)
- SGCH (Senior Grand Champion)
- GFC (Grand Field Champion)
- SGFC (Senior Grand Field Champion)
- WCH (Water Race Champion)
- GWCH (Water Race Grand Champion)
- SGWCH (Senior Grand Water Race Champion)

These titles are used as suffixes:

Obedience
- CD (Companion Dog)
- CDX (Companion Dog Excellent)
- UD (Utility Dog)
- UDX (Utility Dog Excellent)
- VCD1 (Versatile Companion Dog 1)
- VCD2 (Versatile Companion Dog 2)
- VCD3 (Versatile Companion Dog 3)
- VCD4 (Versatile Companion Dog 4)

Tracking Tests
- TD (Tracking Dog)
- TDX (Tracking Dog Excellent)
- VST (Variable Surface Tracker)

Agility Trials
- NA (Novice Agility)
- OA (Open Agility)
- AX (Agility Excellent)
- MX (Master Agility Excellent)
- NAJ (Novice Jumpers with weaves)
- OAJ (Open Jumpers with weaves)
- AXJ (Excellent Jumpers with weaves)
- MXJ (Master Excellent Jumpers with weaves)

Hunting Test
- JH (Junior Hunter)
- SH (Senior Hunter)
- MH (Master Hunter)

Herding Test
- HT (Herding Tested)
- PT (Pre-Trial Tested)
- HS (Herding Started)
- HI (Herding Intermediate)
- HX (Herding Excellent)

Lure Coursing
- JC (Junior Courser)
- SC (Senior Courser)
- MC (Master Courser)

Earthdog
- JE (Junior Earthdog)
- SE (Senior Earthdog)
- ME (Master Earthdog)

Lure Coursing
- JC (Junior Courser)
- SC (Senior Courser)
- MC (Master Courser)

EARNING AGILITY TITLES

The first organization to promote agility trials in the US was the United States Dog Agility Association, Inc. (USDAA), which was established in 1986 and spawned numerous member clubs around the country. Both the USDAA and the AKC offer titles to winning dogs. Three titles are available through the USDAA: Agility Dog (AD), Advanced Agility Dog (AAD) and Master Agility Dog (MAD). The AKC offers Novice Agility (NA), Open Agility (OA), Agility Excellent (AX) and Master Agility Excellent (MX). Beyond these four AKC titles, dogs can win additional ones in "jumper" classes, Jumpers with Weave Novice (NAJ), Open (OAJ) and Excellent (MXJ), which lead to the ultimate title(s): MACH, Master Agility Champion. Dogs can continue to add number designations to the MACH titles, indicating how many times the dog has met the MACH requirements, such as MACH1, MACH2 and so forth.

(Novice Brace Draft Dog), and BDD (Brace Draft Dog).

The BMDCA draft tests, organized as a series of exercises, serve to challenge a Berner's natural working capability for carting or drafting. The draft tests prove a dog's ability to haul a load, requiring both efficiency, successful training and the dog's natural aptitude for the work. The breed inherits a zeal for hauling, and drafting dogs show great willingness and joy in pulling. The exercises in the draft tests represents real-life work situations, all of which represent some historical function of the breed. The regulation for draft tests abide by the same rules as the AKC's obedience trials.

VERSATILITY AND WORKING DOG AWARDS

Is there any doubt that the Bernese Mountain Dog is a versatile breed? Certainly not in the eyes of the parent club, as the BMDCA offers a Versatility Award to any dog that wins a Champion title in the show ring, a Novice Draft Dog title plus one other title (obedience, tracking, agility or herding). There are hundreds of Berners who have earned the award.

The Working Dog Award and the Working Dog Excellent Award, both offered by the BMDCA, are designed to recognize versatile Berners that carry on the breed's original purpose. The Working Dog Award is given to dogs that earn the Novice Draft Dog title plus two of the following: Companion Dog, Tracking Dog or Junior Herding Dog/Novice Agility/Novice Agility Jumper. The Working Dog Excellent Award is given to dogs with the Draft Dog title, as well as two of the following: Companion Dog Excellent, Tracking Dog Excellent/Variable Surface Tracker or Open Agility/Open Agility Jumpers.

INDEX

My Bernese Mountain Dog

PUT YOUR PUPPY'S FIRST PICTURE HERE

Dog's Name _____

Date _____ Photographer _____